KU-064-335

PRAISE FOR *FREEDOM SEEKER*

'Freedom Seeker *is a modern-day manifesto for those who seek to make the journey from trampled and trapped to alive and free.'*

JONATHAN FIELDS, AUTHOR OF *HOW TO LIVE A GOOD LIFE* AND FOUNDER, GOOD LIFE PROJECT

'Women too often find themselves trapped by their own expectations, the expectations of others, and the pursuit of conventional – often materialistic – success. As they become increasingly imprisoned and weighed down by obligations, guilt, rules and the pressures of modern life, women see their early potential and ideals evaporate. Freedom Seeker *offers a way out: an invaluable road-map to help women recognize the problem, trust their own instincts and, ultimately, break free.'*

CAROL BELLAMY, FORMER EXECUTIVE DIRECTOR OF UNICEF

'We live in times when building a career on our core values and vision (rather than on ones being dictated to us), is becoming increasingly possible. Beth is one of the pioneers in this new heady world of escapees and freedom seekers. The misconception that seeking freedom or escaping is running away from reality couldn't be further from the truth. Seeking freedom is finding one's true north. It is a struggle, and one of the most important journeys you'll ever take. Beth is the perfect guide for your most important quest yet.'

BEN KEENE, HEAD OF THE ESCAPE SCHOOL, FOUNDER OF TRIBEWANTED & REBEL BOOK CLUB

'The search for a life we will love, not a life we have 'done', is not always linear. Enter Freedom Seeker and with it a safe pair of hands, a fresh new voice and above all, a well-lit path to find your way. Part toolbox, part wise tome and many a hilarious, honest missive in between, Beth Kempton's Freedom Seeker *is a correction of the flawed reliance on the generic prescription of "happy... now!" Instead this book takes you on a personal journey to find your own curvy, bumpy line to your true self, and what you love.'*

SARAH DICKINSON, CO-FOUNDER & MANAGING DIRECTOR, THNK THE SCHOOL OF CREATIVE LEADERSHIP

'Beth Kempton is a warrior against cynicism. In her quest to find the keys to freedom, Beth has found many inspirational tales of other people breaking the chains of routine and finding the path to a better life. Impossible to be cynical about that!'

OLLIE STONE-LEE, BBC RADIO 4 TODAY PROGRAMME

'In Freedom Seeker, Beth Kempton examines the intricacies of a complex universal experience that often goes agonizingly unspoken: feeling trapped. Through personal reflection and shared stories, she opens our eyes to transformative ways to discover – or rediscover – the feeling of what it means to be free. With each chapter Beth graciously hands us the very keys to open our own cages, allowing us to liberate ourselves, unfurl our wings and fly!'

TRACEY CLARK, AUTHOR OF ELEVATE THE EVERYDAY: A PHOTOGRAPHIC GUIDE TO PICTURING MOTHERHOOD

'It is seldom you get to read something so beautifully written and filled with immeasurable and unconditional inspiration as Freedom Seeker. Not only will you read Beth Kempton's book once, you will underline the words that speak to you, memorize the passages that are vital to your wellbeing, and read it again and again when you are wandering or lost and need a friend to help you find your way. It is an honour for me to highly recommend, even insist, that you add it to the list of well-read books in your library.'

JO PACKHAM, EDITOR-IN-CHIEF, WHERE WOMEN CREATE, WHERE WOMEN COOK & WHERE WOMEN CREATE BUSINESS

'Although I already do what I love, there are still times I want to "live more and worry less. Freedom Seeker came at just the right moment. With practical and inspiring tasks Beth helped me think about what matters most in life. She showed me how to free myself from my daily routine, be more aware of the choices I have and make life more fulfilling and inspirational.'

IRENE SMIT, CREATIVE DIRECTOR, FLOW MAGAZINE

'Freedom Seeker speaks to the expansive spirit in all of us that sometimes gets crushed by the pressures of daily life, or suppressed by fear. This book will show you how to liberate that spirit, and be truly happy living in alignment with your heart.'

AMY BUTLER, DESIGNER, AUTHOR AND CREATOR OF BLOSSOM MAGAZINE

'When I quit my corporate job to pursue my passions I thought I'd automatically freed myself from the cage of external expectations. But just like with Beth Kempton's story and those of her featured Freedom Seekers, I needed to define what freedom really meant to me so I could eventually free myself. Beth's tested framework and Freedom Keys serve as a valuable guide and companion on the journey to finding your flock and taking flight.'

JENNIFER LEE, AUTHOR OF THE RIGHT-BRAIN BUSINESS PLAN

'So there I was. Fluent speaker of Japanese, interpreter for royalty and elite athletes. I'd gaily tackled conferences with world leaders, but I was in a crumpled heap, feeling utterly overwhelmed by my own tiny baby. Odd, isn't it, that the whole new world of possibilities that comes with giving birth can actually make a new mother feel trapped. It wasn't until a long time later that I managed to re-learn from my children the art of existing in the moment. How I wish Beth had crafted this book years ago, so I could have learned the secrets of her Freedom Keys and managed to learn how to feel free in the moment much, much earlier. In a book that is truly supportive and brimming over with personal anecdotes, Freedom Seeker will help you discover how to become the best version of yourself. Just like on a plane, when you should fit your own oxygen mask before assisting children, you can't help others until you've sorted yourself out. In this book Beth has given us a feather on our paths, to remind us to pause, and help us become infectiously magnificent: the best example for our children.'

- HILARY FRANK, MAYOR OF SALTASH (WHO, BLESSED WITH BETH'S FRIENDSHIP, STILL LOVES JUMPING IN MUDDY PUDDLES)

'Life doesn't always turn out how we expect or hope. Freedom Seeker provides the tools to recalibrate how you look at your life journey, and break free from the constraints of your subconscious mind so you can soar.'

LEYLA HUTCHINGS, TRUSTEE, SURROGACY UK

'Freedom Seeker made me truly appreciate that I am the one person who can unburden myself of any constraints that I have unconsciously placed on myself over the years. This book is empowering and uplifting.'

CAROL COUSE, SPORTS LAWYER

'As someone who cares deeply about making a difference in the world while also being incredibly career driven, I found Freedom Seeker a go-to for approaches, perspectives and solutions for taking the next steps in my life. The stories and advice are amazing tools for those struggling to find the right balance personally and professionally.'

ALEXANDRA CHALAT, WORLD ECONOMIC FORUM GLOBAL SHAPER, BUSINESSWOMAN, SPORTS AND SOCIAL CHANGE SPECIALIST

'Freedom Seeker reveals an uplifting and vulnerable journey. Each step of the way I was left with a sense of freedom to truly live into my soul's calling and desire. A brilliant book.'

LARA TABATZNIK, FOUNDER, 42 ACRES

'Beth knows all about achieving astonishing success, but she also understands that even in the midst of outward accomplishments, one can feel trapped in a cage of responsibilities. There is often a need to recalibrate and get back to a sense of freedom. This is the perfect guide for that. I wish I had had a book like this at various junctures in my own career!'

LILLA ROGERS, FOUNDER, LILLA ROGERS STUDIO

FREEDOM

SEEKER

Live More. Worry Less.
Do What You Love.

Beth Kempton

HAY HOUSE

Carlsbad, California • New York City • London
Sydney •Johannesburg • Vancouver • New Delhi

First published and distributed in the United Kingdom by:
Hay House UK Ltd, Astley House, 33 Notting Hill Gate, London W11 3JQ
Tel: +44 (0)20 3675 2450; Fax: +44 (0)20 3675 2451; www.hayhouse.co.uk

Published and distributed in the United States of America by:
Hay House Inc., PO Box 5100, Carlsbad, CA 92018-5100
Tel: (1) 760 431 7695 or (800) 654 5126; Fax: (1) 760 431 6948 or (800) 650 5115
www.hayhouse.com

Published and distributed in Australia by:
Hay House Australia Ltd, 18/36 Ralph St, Alexandria NSW 2015
Tel: (61) 2 9669 4299; Fax: (61) 2 9669 4144; www.hayhouse.com.au

Published and distributed in the Republic of South Africa by:
Hay House SA (Pty) Ltd, PO Box 990, Witkoppen 2068
info@hayhouse.co.za; www.hayhouse.co.za

Published and distributed in India by:
Hay House Publishers India, Muskaan Complex, Plot No.3, B-2,
Vasant Kunj, New Delhi 110 070
Tel: (91) 11 4176 1620; Fax: (91) 11 4176 1630; www.hayhouse.co.in

Distributed in Canada by:
Raincoast Books, 2440 Viking Way, Richmond, B.C. V6V 1N2
Tel: (1) 604 448 7100; Fax: (1) 604 270 7161; www.raincoast.com

Text © Beth Kempton, 2017

The moral rights of the author have been asserted.

All rights reserved. No part of this book may be reproduced by any mechanical, photographic or electronic process, or in the form of a phonographic recording; nor may it be stored in a retrieval system, transmitted or otherwise be copied for public or private use, other than for 'fair use' as brief quotations embodied in articles and reviews, without prior written permission of the publisher.

The information given in this book should not be treated as a substitute for professional medical advice; always consult a medical practitioner. Any use of information in this book is at the reader's discretion and risk. Neither the author nor the publisher can be held responsible for any loss, claim or damage arising out of the use, or misuse, of the suggestions made, the failure to take medical advice or for any material on third party websites.

A catalogue record for this book is available from the British Library.

ISBN: 978-1-78180-805-4

Interior illustrations: Liam Frost

Printed and bound by CPI Group (UK) Ltd, Croydon, CR0 4YY

For Sienna and Maia,
May you always fly free.

CONTENTS

PROLOGUE

I used to think Freedom lived on the open road, windows rolled down, music turned up.

In my imagination she was a curious explorer and a soulful seeker of beauty.

She roamed happily through faraway lands, hair braided with flowers and pockets filled with stardust.

She ate wonder for breakfast and adrenalin for lunch. Adventure was like breathing to her. Spontaneous. Essential.

I was 20. Of course I knew. Freedom was my daring travel companion on the thrilling ride of life.

Looking back, I'm not quite sure when we parted company. I can't pinpoint the exact moment that she was lost to the archives of memory. There wasn't a major crisis that sent her away. It was more like a gradual fading from my everyday awareness, until one day I realized she was gone.

I have been seeking Freedom ever since.

Where is she when you become a parent, spouse, cog in the wheel of business and society? When career pressures steal your precious days? Or you get turned upside down by the demands of children? When money is tight and stress runs high? When you have to battle with an illness or be there as others suffer?

Where is she when the voice in your head says your dreams are too big, or it's too late to start? When the people who care for you most tell you that passion won't pay the bills? And who are you to have those dreams anyway?

What about when adventure feels like a long-ago luxury? And doing what you love seems selfish and impractical? Where is she then?

We often build our lives in a way that shuts out Freedom. We fill our days with work, our ears with noise and our cupboards with stuff. We weigh ourselves down with worries, debts, obligations, other people's pain. We make assumptions and blindly follow fashions. We don't break enough rules.

We chase the kind of success that ultimately holds us back. What we thought we wanted isn't actually making us happy. We often listen to the wrong people, when we should be listening to ourselves.

This book is the result of many years of searching, of seeking my old friend Freedom, through the life-changing impact of marriage, the trials of motherhood and the pressures of running my own business.

And here's what I have discovered: I was looking in the wrong place all along.

Freedom is actually found within, in the shape of our laughter and the way we love, in the truths that we live by and the stories we become. She is a light heart, a clear head, a gentle smile. She wanders in the landscape of the mind, and nourishes the deepest yearnings of the soul.

She is me. I am her.

But here's the thing. Sometimes life happens and we are split in two. Part of us gets trapped in a cage – surrounded by bars of guilt, worry, obligation, exhaustion and more. The good news is that the other part of us is always free, even if it doesn't feel that way. The key is recognizing when you are trapped, and then knowing how to escape whatever life sends your way.

You might manage to escape one cage only to find another cage closing in on you. This cycle of imprisonment and escape is a corollary of human growth; every time we get trapped and free ourselves, we learn a little, grow a little. But being trapped feels hard and escape tastes better.

Any time you feel like you are in a cage, this book will help you locate your free self and find your way back to whole again. Looking for her is a choice. Finding her is a choice. Giving her reasons to stay is a choice.

The truth is, feeling free is a choice that is ours for the making, ours for the taking at any time, at any age.

This book is to remind you what it's like to feel free, and offers a host of practical tools to help you escape.

From one Freedom Seeker to another, my wish for you is that you will find whatever you need to set yourself free.

Let's head out on this adventure together, and find our way home.

Chapter 1

CAGED BIRD: YOUR INVITATION TO ESCAPE

I know what freedom tastes like, and when I'm trapped the flashbacks come easily…

I lasted less than 15 minutes on horseback. It was the way my borrowed steed nearly sent me cascading over the cliff edge with each sultry curve of the mountain path, rump heaving from side to side as she clip-clopped along.

My stomach was already delicate from the highly spiced yak curry I had unexpectedly shared with the Prince of Bhutan the night before. As I dismounted and began the rest of the climb to the hallowed Tiger's Nest Monastery on foot, I reflected on my surreal brush with royalty.

I was in the Land of the Thundering Dragon at the invitation of my old friend Hidetoshi Nakata. He's a smart, sweet, Italian-speaking

Japanese guy who happens to be a really famous football player. I used to be his English teacher, but that's another story.

The Bhutanese love football. Young monks roll up old robes to make their own kickabout in the dusty shadows of ancient temples. Children play on street corners, with shirts for goalposts. Taxi drivers stop a moment to say, 'You know David Beckham?' before handing over your change. So being in Bhutan with one of Asia's sporting heroes was always going to bring some surprises.

The forlorn horse had gone on ahead with my guide Namgay, and I stopped for a while to stand alone, breathing deeply at the edge of the mountain. A gentle mist tumbled over the rice paddies of the Paro Valley nearly 1,000 metres below. Ahead was nothingness: just a vast expanse of hazy sky, and a few clouds perching on the shoulders of the monastery. The complex of white temple buildings gripped the mountainside, prayer flags stretched across the chasm like a confident tightrope walker showing off.

It was silent up there. And high. So high. The mist moved in, so close I could taste it. Legend has it that Guru Rinpoche flew there on the back of a tigress 1,300 years ago, and meditated in the caves for three years before introducing the Bhutanese to Buddhism. I didn't doubt it. I was half expecting the tigress to lope out of one of the caves, lick her paws and steal away.

I was filled up by that holy place, the monastery in the sky. And yet I was as light as the prayer flags rippling in the breeze. There was magic in the air, and it was as if I were inhaling the very breath of the flying tiger herself.

That feeling of freedom was as precious as a fortune waiting to be told.

It's that girl who flashes across my mind, eight years later, as I collapse on my bedroom floor, exhausted, tears streaming down my face, shoulders heaving, a shattered mess. My baby is crying, my pregnant belly is heavy, my jeans don't fit and I am unprepared for the public speaking appearance scheduled for later that night. All I want to do is crawl into bed and sleep for days.

I had gone to Bhutan on a whim, I remember. I had been planning a work visit to India when my friend Hide mentioned he was visiting the ancient kingdom. I remember thinking that it was pretty cool when HRH Prince Jigyel Ugyen Wangchuck rocked up for dinner, but I'm not sure I considered how unusual it was that we spent the evening chatting about our love lives, fashion and fishing, and ditched protocol to hug goodbye.

Through my tears I see that holy mountain, mist descending over a tiny figure whose eyes are shining with delight, her heart cracked open and wonder pouring in. Who is she, this brave, cheerful adventurer who has just dined with the brother of the Dragon King?

Then more flashbacks...

Who is this girl riding the Trans-Siberian Railway with a carriage-full of chandelier-toting Chinese merchants? This laughing creature climbing the Great Wall of China in flip-flops because she forgot her walking shoes in her excited rush to catch the bus? Who is this nature-loving explorer drinking G&T on the rocks, made with ice she chipped off an Antarctic iceberg, captivated by a twirling humpback whale? This innocent sky-gazer watching the New Year moon rise over the Sahara Desert? This spontaneous adventurer who is happy to talk to anyone, go anywhere, try anything?

She, my friend, is me, before I watched my whole world shrink to this bedroom floor. You know, I feel bad saying that. I feel guilty even thinking it. I know I must sound selfish and ungrateful, but it's the truth, and when everything else has fallen away, the truth is all that's left.

In the chaos of nappy changing, toddler tantrums and work deadlines, some days I hardly recognize that girl. In fact, I look in the mirror and hardly recognize my own face, with the deep furrow above my brow, dark circles beneath my eyes, and baby weight that just won't leave me alone. At least I've washed my hair today.

But now, clarity. I realize that it's up to me. I get to choose, and this caged bird wants to fly free.

AN INVITATION

This book is an invitation to seek freedom in every corner of your life. It's about living more, worrying less and finding a way to do what you love every day. It sounds simple, and in some ways it is, but when you are trapped in a cage with broken wings, freedom can seem like a far away deeply buried treasure. I know, because I've been there. Many times.

Most importantly, I want you to know that you are not alone. Freedom Seekers everywhere are feeling this way. I know that many, many people all over the world are feeling the same suffocation, inertia, guilt and pain. I've seen it in the eyes of strangers in the street, overheard it in the gaps in conversations, felt it in the words of friends and observed it in the discussions in my online community.

Deep down we all know that freedom is a choice and a human right. Yet millions of us don't feel that truth. We feel trapped by our circumstances, relationships, social pressures, financial status and education. Caged by our expectations of ourselves, and others' expectations of us, and by our beliefs, doubts and fears.

We allow ourselves to be held back from living our fullest lives. Individually it is heartbreaking. Collectively it is a colossal waste of potential. Together we are going to change this. In finding the courage and confidence to escape our cages and shine, we will help others do the same.

My personal story isn't a dramatic one of hitting rock bottom. That's not how it happened. Mine is one of a slow ebbing of joy from my days, of stemming that flow and finding myself again, the present-day version of me, in love with the life I've got.

I'll also share the stories of people whose cage doors have been slammed in their faces, the darkness pushing them right to the edge, before they had no choice but escape. Theirs are high-velocity, adrenalin-pumping truths about how freedom seeking saved their lives.

Whichever kind of story you identify with, there are valuable lessons in each and every one. I hope they will show you it's fine not to know exactly what the future holds, but it's within your power to play an active role in shaping it.

FEELING TRAPPED

You are reading this because your heart knows there is a greater version of your life available to you. The version where you feel free. Whatever your reason for being trapped, we're going to get you out.

The opposite of happy is not always unhappy. It can be a vague greyness that is hard to pin down. A muffled rumble, where laughter used to be. It's hard to put into words, because we don't really speak of it.

In a world where statistically we are among the most privileged, it can be difficult to talk about feeling trapped. You know how it goes. 'Why would you moan about your steady job? At least you have one.' 'Why would you complain about your partner? At least you have one.' We compare ourselves to others, presuming that having something is better than not having it, allowing our real and valid concerns to be diminished by those two tiny but crushing words, 'at least'.

Sure we need to be grateful, but it's dangerous to be grateful for the wrong things, for the wrong reasons. If you're trapped in a cage, you don't want to start being grateful for the protection of the bars. You need to be grateful that there are gaps in between them so you can see what's on the other side.

We dream of escape and of taking flight, of navigating our own path through open skies and of living happily ever after. Yet we often feel powerless to make it happen. We know that we need to change something, but feel so disconnected from our free selves that we're not even sure what we actually want. This book is an invitation to sift through those thoughts and feelings to find your way out.

Escape is a process, not a pill. The journey of the Freedom Seeker isn't always easy. But it is essential, and it is urgent, for it is the path to coming alive again. It's a long road, and it will be uncomfortable in places, but we're going to travel it together.

I have lived every page of this book. In the writing of it I have danced and tumbled, laughed and crumbled, cried, shrunk, grown, travelled thousands of miles, talked to strangers, looked deep inside myself and rediscovered my own stories. I have centred myself and fallen apart, many times over.

I have screamed at the noise and revelled in the silence. I have followed the sun, howled at the moon, and sent thanks to the stars. I have talked to hundreds of women and a good number of men who have shared stories I will never forget.

I hope I have gathered the best of it all, the most powerful lessons and inspiring tales to show that if I can do it, and they can do it, then you too can do it.

The writing of this book has made me feel more deeply connected, vital and alive than I have in years. I hope in reading it, and in the living of it, you too find a way to inhale the magic and mystery and beauty of your own life, wherever you are, however old you are, whoever you are.

WHAT IS FREEDOM ANYWAY?

In over two decades of seeking, I have come to understand this: **Freedom is the willingness and ability to choose your own path and experience your life as your true self.**

Whatever circumstances we are born into, wherever we live, whatever we believe, we all have the innate capacity to feel free. Why? It is part of who we are, in the same way that love is our essential nature.

But over time life happens, we find ourselves in difficult situations, and sometimes our reactions take over. Our thoughts about a given situation, our emotional response to it, and the stories we tell ourselves about what is going on expand as we give them attention. Eventually they fill our minds, solidifying into cage bars and trapping us inside. The good news is if you can choose your way into the cage, you can choose your way out.

While you cannot always change your situation, you can always change the way you respond to it.

This is a book about personal freedom, not liberty. There is an important distinction. Liberty is about BEING free and is granted by laws and conventions and government permissions. Freedom, as used in this book, is about FEELING free, and the only permission you need for that is your own.

MAPPING YOUR ESCAPE

In each chapter you'll find exercises to help you assimilate the concepts and move forwards in your own journey. I encourage you to find a dedicated notebook to record each step. By the end, when you look back, you will be staggered how far you have travelled.

Some of the exercises will push you to dig deep. Find some quiet, and listen to what you really want to say. Be gentle on yourself. If any part of any exercise is too painful, come back to it later, or get some support to help you investigate, but don't stop reading. Something may shift as the words sink in.

Above all else, be honest. No one is watching. This is for you. You can do it.

Entry 1:
Your commitment to freedom seeking

Copy out the text below, then sign and date it. If you like, make your own beautiful version, or download a template from www.bethkempton.com/flyfree and stick it on the wall, somewhere you will see it every day.

I am a Freedom Seeker and I choose to feel free.

I am willing and able to choose my own path.

I am committed to experiencing my life as my true self.

THE REALITY OF ESCAPE

The figure of a bird escaping from a cage has symbolized the fear and bravery of the human condition for just as long as there have been birdcages. But to me the metaphor falls short. It suggests just an in or out, cage or no cage, trapped or free. But that's not how it works.

We aren't afraid or brave, we're usually both. We don't suddenly flee a cage. At first we might not even know it's there, and when we finally notice the bars and open the door, we often have no idea where to go. And the vast expanse beyond the door can be terrifying. Sometimes we have spent so long in the cage that it feels safer to remain inside.

This book will guide you out the door, encouraging you to throw yourself deep into the experience of your own life. More importantly it will implore you to do it as the real you, layers peeled back, nothing hidden.

We will take a step back to understand how so many of us get stuck in the first place. We'll dig deep into the social norms and assumptions about what's 'best for us', and question why those things aren't making us happy. I want you to challenge the need always to do what is expected of you, or what you feel you 'should' do, in favour of doing what feels right.

Please make time and space for this book in your life, because there is no better reason to get up in the morning than to spend your day doing what you love, and no greater prize than feeling free.

Question everything. Disrupt the status quo. Forget the status quo and start over, if that's what you need to do.

Break the rules. Make the rules. Have no rules. This is your journey.

Remember, you get to choose.

Does a seeker ever actually find what they are looking for, or is the reward in the quest? That, my friend, is for you to discover.

Freedom seeking is big. It's bold. And it might just save your life.

WHY ME?

It's ironic that we often become imprisoned by our greatest gifts – family, children, relationships, career opportunities, our own success. Through my own journey, I have come to discover how it is possible to escape the cage without sacrificing those gifts.

I am just an ordinary person from an ordinary family, but I've been blessed with some extraordinary experiences because I chose to be a Freedom Seeker. Here's how it all began, when I escaped my first cage two decades ago – an experience that has shaped the rest of my life.

While most of the other 17-year-olds I knew were down the pub drinking cider, clutching their fake IDs and gossiping about the latest indie rock band, I was on a boat in the middle of the Bay of Biscay, having a light-bulb moment.

Up until that point I'd been a curious teenager who loved to learn, but had never ventured far from home. I narrowly avoided the 'geek' label by regularly trading my maths homework with the cool kids for the chance to hang out with them at lunch. I was a straight-A student on track to do Economics at Cambridge. Not because I was any kind of genius, but because I was a hard worker with a sharp memory who had a knack for answering exam questions.

After that, I was going to train as an accountant because I'd been told to aim for a stable career with a good salary. It was all mapped out. My parents and teachers encouraged this safe choice because they believed it would serve me well. And to be fair, I thought it was what I wanted. I saw the nice cars and smart suits. I liked the idea of a business card with an impressive job title and company logo. I imagined myself jetting around the world to client meetings, staying in swanky hotels and dining out in fancy restaurants.

I clearly hadn't thought it through, because I now know that the day-to-day reality of being an accountant wouldn't have suited me at all. But there were enough people suggesting it, and enough reasons to go along with it, that I didn't veer from 'The Plan'.

Until, that is, I got the opportunity to join a crew racing a sail training yacht in The Cutty Sark Tall Ships' Race from the UK to Spain. I paid for it with my savings, boosted by the proceeds of endless car washing and sponsored swims. I had only been abroad once, and never without my parents, so this was a massive leap for me.

The Bay of Biscay had a thrillingly dangerous reputation, and I actually drafted a will, which I hid in the desk in my bedroom before I left, just in case. My older brother would get my Sony Walkman. My younger brother would get my bike.

A couple of days into the race, after long night-watches and some hairy weather, a blue sky opened up and we sailed into an area of complete calm. I was at the helm alone, while everyone else slept below or lazed on the foredeck. I felt like I had an entire ocean to myself, with only a chirpy school of dolphins for company. As they splashed around the bow, I looked out to sea and let out a deep, contented sigh. The sun was shining and there was so much space all around. I felt as if I had been holding my breath for years, and only then exhaled.

Three things hit me like a lightning bolt:

1. I didn't want to be an accountant.

2. I had absolutely no idea what I wanted to do with my life (and that was kind of exciting).

3. I wanted to feel how I felt in that moment for the rest of my days.

How did I feel in that moment? I felt happy. I felt deeply connected to the planet, extended beyond myself, part of the waves and the sky and the beauty of it all. I felt called to explore. I was out there dancing with the dolphins. I felt free.

In that flash of clarity, I knew I wanted a life full of adventure. This revelation was at once terrifying and electrifying. I had painted a particular picture of what I thought I should be striving for and had been holding onto that for years. But in that one moment of lucidity, I realized I had been completely wrong about myself.

It was as if the sun's rays had bounced off my cage, revealing bars that had previously been invisible. I had been trapped by expectation, a sense of duty, an inevitability about my career path. I was incarcerated by a drive for material success before my career had even begun.

I wanted out.

I decided to eschew the well-trodden career path, ignore the rules and get off the quick road to financial reward. I made the choice to seek freedom and do things my way. In that moment the cage door swung open and I saw a whole world outside.

For the remainder of that trip my senses were on high alert. I couldn't get enough of nature, the sun, wind and stars. In port I partied hard all night long.

And then I returned home and had to rethink everything. The truth is I didn't have a plan. I was much clearer about what I didn't want than what I did, but that was still good information. Answering the question 'What shall I do with my life?' seemed too big for a teenager fresh back from an a-ha moment, so I focused my efforts on choosing an alternative undergraduate course.

At the time I was studying A-levels in Maths, Further Maths, Economics, Physics and General Studies. Most people take three subjects. I was killing myself with five. So I dropped one, and promised myself than when I finished my exams I would be done with academic subjects.

Instead I wanted to learn something that was going to take me on an adventure. Opting for a degree that would give me a year abroad seemed like the answer. I loved the idea of connecting with people in far-off lands, and discovering more about the world. However, I hadn't studied any languages at A-level – a prerequisite to all modern language degrees at the time. Except, that is, if you chose something obscure and insanely difficult, like Chinese, Japanese, Russian or Arabic.

Although popular now, in 1994 learning these languages was the domain of talented linguists. I couldn't speak a word of any of them; I could hardly even speak French. So I did what any slightly reckless teenager might do and used the nursery rhyme 'Eeny Meeny Miny Moe' to make the most significant decision of my life. I landed on Japanese, and in that moment left my cage behind.

As it turns out, there was no pushback from my parents or teachers, because they saw me come alive that summer. Japanese wasn't easy. But I worked at it, and soon fell in love with the language and culture.

Looking back, I can see that everything that has happened since can be traced back to that moment on the boat, and the people I have met along the way. That single decision led me to many rich experiences I could never have planned, simply because I chose to be a Freedom Seeker.

It's not like I escaped that cage and have felt free every day since, as I've been trapped and escaped several times over. What I now know is that I used my Freedom Keys – a unique and powerful tool that I will share with you in this book – to get out and fly free each time.

THE FREEDOM KEYS

Over the past six years I have ushered thousands of people out the doors of their respective cages. My company, Do What You Love, runs online courses, workshops and retreats that encourage personal enquiry, creativity and exploration into making your passion pay. I've helped people all over the world find personal, professional and financial freedom doing what they love

But when I started out producing these courses, I didn't actually realize it was about freedom. I always focused on the concept of 'doing what you love', having a fundamental belief that we are happier when we explore our passions and magic happens when we follow our dreams. I believed that we become fuller versions of ourselves when we do something that lights us up, and that is better for everyone.

I still believe that, but after six years and a cascade of course graduates' stories of transformation, I have come to see that actually it was always about freedom. Doing what you love is one way to travel, but the destination is feeling free.

When we're trapped, freedom can seem like a luxury reserved for other people, a concept we think we know but can't quite remember. Even then, when flying free seems far removed from our current reality, we want to believe that today can be better than yesterday. That tomorrow can be better than today. That life in the cage isn't all there is. Our current state of living isn't a life sentence. At the very least, we no longer want to feel trapped, crushed, small. We all want to escape.

> *Freedom is the Holy Grail. We want to feel that we have the power to direct our own lives, choose our path and consciously manifest our own happiness.*

So I got curious. I talked to hundreds of people in my community to understand their cages, how they coped and, crucially, how they got out. I also analysed my experiences of incarceration and escape, digging deep for commonalities and recurring themes.

In reverse engineering all these stories, here's what I discovered: Every cage has a door. Every door has a lock. You just need to find the key. It's that simple. At any time, you have the power to set yourself free.

There is a very clear pattern to escape – it appears in every single story, in every single situation, with every single person – and it led me to identify a set of eight principles that I call 'the Freedom Keys', which can unlock the door of **any** cage. This tool is my gift to you.

It's not about finding a cure for guilt, jealousy, stress, resentment or whatever else your cage bars represent. It's about taking your mind to a place where those things don't get any attention – the place where your free self lives.

Whatever is trapping you, however dark the space, these Freedom Keys are your ticket to escape.

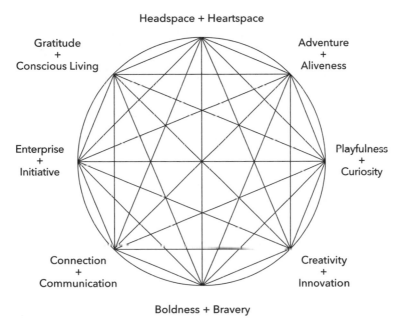

Figure 1: The Freedom Keys

The eight Freedom Keys are:

1. Headspace + Heartspace

2. Adventure + Aliveness

3. Playfulness + Curiosity

4. Creativity + Innovation

5. Boldness + Bravery

6. Connection + Communication

7. Enterprise + Initiative

8. Gratitude + Conscious Living

Not only will these keys unlock your cage, they can guide your flight for the rest of your life.

WHY THE FREEDOM KEYS WORK

I have come to understand that there are two kinds of 'stuckness'. One is deep and black and requires immediate attention. When you are in it, it takes all your effort simply to breathe. It calls to you like a distressed child. Weight. Pressure. Pain. When it all gets too much, your Freedom Keys can provide instant relief.

Then there's the other kind of 'stuckness'. The grey kind, that wisps up to you and wraps around you like a fog, apparently gentle but slowly suffocating you, blurring all the colours out. It sneaks up on you and infiltrates your life gradually, whispering doubts in your ear, taunting you with the things you're afraid of. It siphons off your energy and hope.

This is the silent freedom killer. It's the wasted days in a job you hate, the nodding politely to the horrible boss, the stifling closeness of your daily commute. It's the passing of another birthday, recognizing another year of not very much. It's seeing your friends having the things you want. It's the feeling that you are dragging your feet: eat, work, sleep, repeat, with a few nights out and bottles of wine in between. It's the day you wake up and start to wonder where your old life went.

This kind of stuckness often goes untended, like that dripping tap that never gets fixed. It seems fairly innocuous, but it will drown you if you let it. What you need is a spark to get that fire in your belly lit again – the Freedom Keys are that spark.

Making choices based on your Freedom Keys will lead you in the direction of your passions. Taking immediate action brings instant relief because it takes the focus of your conscious mind away from the cage bars. That action might be big or small. It doesn't matter. It's just a first step. We are trying to get out the door here, not fly across the ocean, not yet anyway. For now just take a step. Any step.

After unlocking the door, the Freedom Keys will then help you set up your life in a way that allows you to feel much freer, every single day. And the freer you are, the freer you become.

We all have ideas about what our lives could be, if only things were different. But when we're trapped – at the point we most need to do something to change things – we often do nothing, because everything feels too hard.

When I'm in the cage I tend to waste a lot of time wishing I felt free and cursing feeling trapped, while doing nothing about it. I dream of wandering through ancient forests in some exotic place, but don't head off for a hike in my local wood. I fantasize about kayaking amongst towering glaciers without renting a canoe on my local river. I daydream about cycling through the vineyards of France, while my bike stays in the garage and I just open a bottle of red.

The Freedom Keys are an antidote to this inertia.

HOW THEY WORK

The eight Freedom Keys are all of equal importance, but some will be more potent for you than others in any given moment. They can be activated individually or in combination, and in any order you choose.

You may find yourself drawn to one particular Freedom Key or a particular pairing. Perhaps you will come to the lock in the dark and have to fumble with all the keys, trying them out one at a time until at last one fits.

Maybe you want to let the keys surprise you. In that case you can simply close your eyes and feel your way to a point on the diagram on page 17, then open your eyes and see where your finger has settled. If you're pointing to one particular key, try that. If you're pointing to a line, notice which Freedom Keys are joined by that line, and try them. If you're pointing to an intersection of lines on the diagram, try all the Freedom Keys connected by those lines. Alternatively, for a bit of fun, try my Random Freedom Key Generating Machine at www.bethkempton.com/flyfree and see what you get.

Be open. Explore. You are Master of the Keys of your cage. Imagine a strong metal ring with eight keys dangling from it. This is the only thing you need to carry with you as you journey forward. As Master of the Keys you have the power to open your cage door anytime you choose, starting now.

A note about the stories in this book

Some of the personal stories in this book are set in far-off lands and involve people who might normally seem out of reach. Some are so extraordinary I wouldn't believe them if I hadn't met these Freedom Seekers myself.

Please don't think you have to be just like them to be inspired by them, or to learn something from them. You just need to know that they are Freedom Seekers too, and we are all more similar and connected than we know.

Along the way I hope you will dig into your own experiences and illustrate the escape process with your own memories, moments and beliefs. Eventually the stories I share will drift aside to make way for your story, the one you are still writing.

Entry 2: Reaching back

Delve into your memories and answer these questions:

1. When was the last time you felt truly free?

2. Where were you?

3. Why were you there?

4. What were you doing?

5. Who were you with? Or were you alone?

6. How did you feel in your body?

7. What was going on in your mind?

8. Who would you be, if you reclaimed the personal power you felt that day?

FINDING YOUR WAY BACK TO FREE

As I described earlier, my most recent experience of being trapped was a perfect storm of growing my own business and having two children just 18 months apart. I didn't love the way I felt that day, and knew I had to make a change before everything imploded. I had to find my way back to free again.

I want to encourage my daughters to grow up kind and strong, loving and adventurous, with big hearts and curious minds. I want to show them how to be that way, by being that way myself. I want to be present for them, in the nurturing and the encouraging, in the dressing up and falling down, in the tears and laughter and all the bits in between. And I want them to know who I am outside of being their mother, inspiring their flight by spreading my own wings.

I am a Freedom Seeker for me and I am a Freedom Seeker for them.

And you, my friend, are a Freedom Seeker too. Just think, what extraordinary experiences could be waiting for you outside your cage?

This book is based on the one simple concept that feeling free is a choice. However difficult that is to hear right now, believe it with all you've got.

As soon as you realize that you get to choose, the whole world opens up.

Happiness is what happens when you forget about trying to be happy, and instead aim to feel free.

Chapter 2

INSIDE OUT: RECOGNIZING YOUR CAGE

When we voice how we are feeling – hemmed in, cut off, slowly going crazy – we often muddle the symptoms and the cause. We know something is wrong, but can't articulate what. And when we're frustrated, exhausted and at our wit's end, our words, intended to open hearts and garner support, often end up creating resentment and hurling blame.

To start talking about it differently, you need to understand that your cage does not hover in a vacuum; it exists in a context.

THE CONTEXT AND THE CAGE

Let me explain. If I imagine myself back in the moment I am having a meltdown on my bedroom floor, there are two things I know for sure:

1. **I am** a mother of two small girls. That's a fact.

2. **I feel** caged by bars of guilt, frustration and stress, and low self-esteem from the lingering baby weight.

What's the difference? The first is a tangible fact about my situation. This is the context in which my life is playing out right now.

The other is intangible emotion. It's psychological. It's a perception. It is about how I *respond* to the context, and the stories I tell myself about it. It's the way I allow my situation to make me feel. It's the way I allow other people to make me feel. This is the **cage**.

The context and the cage are not the same thing. It's like the difference between solitude (a situation) and loneliness (a response to a situation).

We might rage about the context, but it's the cage we need to escape. Feeling trapped by the realities of motherhood doesn't mean I don't want to be a mother. My girls are my bliss and my love for them could power the stars. But perhaps it's because I treasure the context of motherhood so much that I find the cage bars so frustrating. They get in the way of the rest.

Perhaps you hate your job and it's wearing you down, sapping all your energy. The context is that you have a job. The cage is the way you respond to that job, or the stories you tell yourself about it. How you feel frustrated by your boss. The way your energy slips away as you walk through the door. The lack of meaning dragging you down.

Perhaps you feel trapped in a toxic relationship and it's crushing your self-esteem. The context is that you are in a relationship. The cage is the way you respond to that relationship, or the way you're allowing it to make you feel. The way you have started to believe that you're stupid, or worthless, or that you should be grateful, as no one else would have you. The feeling that you have to walk on eggshells. The way the shame shuts you down every time you try to talk to a friend about it.

Recognition of the cage is the first step towards escape, because in acknowledging it, you develop an awareness of the obstacles and the world beyond the bars. This awareness of possibility can lead to a longing so powerful, a vision so inspiring, that eventually you just have to get out.

Entry 3: I am

Suspend judgement and fill in the gaps in the following sentence to describe your role, situation and how you feel about it: 'I am [*role*] who [*your situation*]'. Write as many sentences as you like.

For example:

- *I am... a single mother of four children with a mortgage to pay, who feels like every day is an uphill struggle, and feels like I'm not giving my children what they need.*

- *I am... a father with a good corporate job and a family to support, who dreams of making films but feels that I can't quit because we need the money.*

- *I am… a retired widow with rheumatoid arthritis, who feels physical pain every day and feels sad that I can no longer knit clothes for my grandchildren.*

- *I am… a 30-something woman who has no partner but wants babies, who feels stuck in a job I hate, watching my body clock tick.*

- *I am… a Freedom Seeker in my prime who is shouldering the burden of caring for sick parents, feeling guilty that all I want to do is travel the world and that I resent them for stopping me.*

Note: This exercise only works if you include a description of a person at the beginning of your sentence (such as woman, man, mother, daughter, Australian living in Europe, Freedom Seeker, etc.). For example: *'I am… desperate to be a writer but have no confidence'* is missing 'you' in the sentence.

Now look at your sentences and underline the parts that are facts and unchangeable at this exact point in time. This is your context.

For example: *'I am the mother of a toddler and a baby with no spare time.'* The context is simply that I am 'the mother of a toddler and a baby'. Having 'no spare time' isn't completely true. I don't have *much* spare time, but I don't have *no* spare time. There's a big difference.

What is left of your 'I am…' sentence when you take away the context? What is NOT underlined? This reveals the way you are dealing with or responding to the context, or the stories you are telling yourself about it. These are the bars of your cage.

Note: If you have found yourself writing 'I feel…' instead of 'I am' that is a sure sign that you are talking about your cage, not your context. Even though you might feel that way, it's not a fact about your situation, but rather an observation of your response to it. Make sure you are focusing on the practical facts.

RECOGNIZING THE CAGE

The following story of burnout is one I have heard too many times: different people, different countries, different jobs, but the same downward spiral.

~ Burnout ~

Nicola Moss joined an advertising agency straight out of university, and showed her dedication by arriving early, staying late and often sacrificing her weekends. Despite looking like she had it together at work, at home she would collapse on the sofa, physically and mentally shattered. Then one day, as she arrived at work and went to open the door, she felt strong hands clamping tightly around her neck, squeezing her airway shut. Her whole body tensed, but there was no one else there. Panic was her attacker and he was ferocious.

What happened next was a blessing, as Nicola's boss took her aside and listened while she spilled out everything she had bottled up inside. His wife had experienced a breakdown several years previously, and he knew that the care Nicola received now was critical, and so he arranged for her to take a three-month sabbatical.

Less than three weeks later, after sleeping for 14 days straight, Nicola got on a plane to Bangkok, and over the next few months traversed the world, much of it by train, boat and on foot. Slow travel turned out to be the elixir that nourished her back to life. She has since retrained as a life coach, helping others slow down and avoid burnout.

Burnout happens when we trap ourselves in a cage of expectation, based on society's materialistic, power-driven version of success, our parents' safe version of success, our employer's version of success, or some other version that has nothing to do with what really matters to us.

We attach our self-worth to our work performance or our bank balance or what we look like, and then unsurprisingly we slip into crisis when things go wrong, or we're no longer happy at work, or we put on weight, or the economy tanks and we get laid off. Often it takes years to realize we're even doing this, and it's only then we discover how trapped we actually are. We push ourselves to the limit; afraid of dropping any of the plates we are spinning. But when burnout hits, they all come crashing down.

Too many times something extreme has to happen – like our bodies shutting down as Nicola's did – before we acknowledge what is going on. But ultimately this wake-up call can be a true gift, if we can just see what it is trying to tell us.

The symptoms of incarceration

I surveyed hundreds of people in my community about what being trapped actually feels like, in the mind and in the body. Time and time again they identified similar symptoms. Recognizing them is the first step to release from their stranglehold.

How many of the following are familiar to you?

Body symptoms

- Headaches
- Frown lines
- Nervous tic

- ✿ Bloodshot eyes
- ✿ Bad skin
- ✿ Grinding teeth
- ✿ Aching jaw
- ✿ Drooped head
- ✿ Poor posture
- ✿ Tight shoulders
- ✿ Shallow breathing
- ✿ Weight on chest
- ✿ Palpitations
- ✿ Panic attacks
- ✿ Knotted lump in stomach
- ✿ IBS (Irritable Bowel Syndrome)
- ✿ Bloating
- ✿ Nausea
- ✿ Pain in solar plexus
- ✿ Exhaustion
- ✿ Instability
- ✿ Stress
- ✿ Pressure
- ✿ Muscle tension
- ✿ A feeling of being squashed
- ✿ No energy to move

- Heaviness
- Weakness
- Lethargy
- Sluggish digestion
- Noise sensitivity
- Poor memory
- Insomnia
- Worsening of chronic illness

Mind symptoms

- Soulless feeling
- Not wanting to talk
- No patience
- Anger
- Tornado of thoughts
- Thinking in loops
- Anxiety
- Moodiness
- Detachment
- Feeling like you're swimming against a tide
- Depression or low mood
- Apathy
- Emptiness

Sometimes it helps to know that you aren't the only one. It can also help to know that some of the symptoms may be linked to your life choices because that means you have the capacity to heal yourself.

Entry 4: Look in the mirror

Stand in front of a mirror and imagine you are your free self, looking at your trapped self behind the glass. Ask your trapped self these questions and encourage honest answers:

1. *How are you feeling right now?*
2. *How do you feel in your body?*
3. *What's going on in your head?*
4. *What emotions do you feel regularly?*
5. *How do you currently deal with it and find temporary escape?*
6. *Who else is affected?*
7. *How do they deal with it?*
8. *What would you like to let go of? If you did that right now, how would things be different?*

Now look into the eyes of your trapped self and say this out loud:

'You are not alone. I'm going to get you out.'

'There's a big wide world out here, outside the cage bars.' (If you like, describe the beauty and potential, the vastness and expanse. Tell them how the sun warms your back and the air currents carry you far.)

'You will fly free once more.'

Notice how the face of your trapped self changes as you speak. Perhaps the eyes widen with wonder. Perhaps the frown relaxes a little. Maybe the mouth flickers into a smile.

Remind yourself that YOU just opened the mind, eyes and heart of your trapped self to the possibilities of life outside the cage. And you can do that for yourself again, at any time.

You can use mirrors as a cue to check in with your trapped self anytime. Whenever you catch a glimpse of your reflection – in the hallway, in a shop window, while brushing your teeth – take a moment to have a chat. How are they doing? What do they need to hear right now? How could today be better than yesterday? What might tomorrow bring?

PAIN RESPONSES

Sometimes the emotional pain is so bad that it feels safer to remain in the cage than speak of the pain. At those times, it's important to know this:

There is a difference between experiencing pain and reacting to pain.

Behind the bars you don't have to examine the pain. You can react to it – with anger, frustration, resentment, guilt, or desire for revenge – without actually dealing with it. But allowing yourself to be consumed by your thoughts about the pain is hell and holds you prisoner.

I learned this from a friend who suffered abuse in childhood and was feeling trapped by ongoing anger, guilt and shame. It wasn't until she voiced the truth of her abuse, and examined the facts of the situation, that she could finally start to process it. Dealing with it was hard because, while it made her realize the abuse hadn't been her fault, she also had to acknowledge that one of her parents had allowed it to happen. Understandably this completely changed her relationship with that person. But in the end, it was only in recognizing her cage bars and voicing her truth that she finally set herself free.

When you find yourself in pain, the initial wound is deep and raw. But if you let yourself experience it, and feel it, that wound can heal into a scar. That scarring is real. It is a mark of something that happened to you. It is part of your life experience and your context. In time, while looking at it occasionally might remind you of what you went through, the scar itself won't hurt anymore. But if you remain in the cage and never allow the wound to heal, you leave yourself open to infection and further pain.

FINDING THE GIFT IN THE CONTEXT

Sometimes, oftentimes, life doesn't work out how we expect it to. We find ourselves in contexts we never imagined, dealing with things we have no clue about.

Finding a way to accept the context just for now, even temporarily, and concentrating on finding that feeling of freedom, can make your experience not just more bearable, but actually joyful.

There is a gift in virtually every context. It might be a new opportunity or a chance to reflect, a reason to reconnect with an old friend or a prompt for gratitude. The gifts of parenthood are plenty and obvious – the love, the laughter, the growth, the connection. In a challenging job, the gift might be the friendship of your co-workers, knowing you can pay your bills or getting to work from home on Fridays. Even a context like redundancy can offer a gift, if you're willing to look for it.

∼ A blessing in disguise ∼

Take Kerry Roy, for example. Kerry was made redundant in 2012, and her immediate reaction was one of disappointment and a feeling of unworthiness. But Kerry was not the kind of person to wallow for long. She saw an opportunity for a fresh start, and realized she finally had the time to explore a big idea she'd been toying with for years – to create the perfect glamping site.

Kerry negotiated a lease for a site nestled within a beautiful 250-acre estate in Yorkshire, in the north of England. She used her redundancy settlement and equity from her house to set up Camp Kátur, named after the Icelandic word for 'happy'. The company mantra is 'Discover your outdoor happiness,' which is fitting indeed, as by seeing the blessing of her redundancy, Kerry had done just that herself.

Sometimes it's hard to find the gift. Sometimes it's hard even to imagine that there might actually be one. But I promise you, there is. This isn't the same as saying, 'everything happens for a reason' but rather 'this is happening, and I'm going to find a way through'.

In some cases the most important gift might be the realization that you never want to experience something again, or the recognition of your own strength to have survived so much for so long. In my case, the wake-up call I described earlier made me determined to handle my second pregnancy, birth and maternity leave very differently to how I 'handled' things first time round.

You can look at your context as one particular aspect of your life that is challenging, or you can look at your whole life as one context, and seek gifts there. You are alive. You are still young, even if only in spirit. Perhaps you have a loving family or precious dreams that keep you going.

Even just believing that there might be a gift, and actively searching for it, can be enough to cause a shift. However deeply buried it may be, knowing it is there can help you accept the facts of your current situation and ease your response to it.

～ Seeing the gift ～

Lisa McArthur-Edwards, a brave woman in one of my online classes, was confined to her house with chronic back pain. During the course she came to realize the difference between the pain itself and her frustration and anger about the pain.

Thinking differently about her context, she started to see gifts in it, like how she felt loved when her friends rallied round to help. She started looking for things she could do, instead of getting hung up on what she couldn't. She could drive, so adventure was still accessible, even if more logistically challenging than before. As a result she ventured out for the first time in months and is now setting up an online business so she can come off sick leave and work from home.

Entry 5: Find the gift

Look at the context you described in Entry 3 (see page 25) and search for a gift in it. If you can't find one, widen your context. What else is true about your current situation? I promise you there is a gift in there somewhere. If you're really stuck, ask someone else what they see.

Write this gift out and post it somewhere you can see it every day to remind you of what you can be grateful for, even when times are challenging.

If you like, share it on social media using the hashtag #freedomseeker so I can see it too.

HIDING BEHIND BARS

Ironically we sometimes find comfort in the cage. We can go deep into the detail of the difficulty over and over – especially if we are surrounded by people who focus on worry and suffering. We can get addicted to sympathy, even revel in the attention. And if we have a secret identity we've been hiding, it's almost always easier in the short term to remain inside the secret than to share it.

When we start believing our own stories, they reverberate from all directions, and we reinforce a version of ourselves that is not the whole truth. There is a danger in telling a tale of woe so many times that we end up not knowing who we are without it. We are afraid of what might be lost when we release it, forgetting to consider what might be found if we do.

Many of us feel a false sense of security in accepting limited options. We cling to what we know, or what we think we 'should' do within the sphere we inhabit, even when it is inhibiting us. We overthink the impact of the answers instead of sinking deeply into the questions. In this paradox of protection, we tend to look outward for advice rather than inward, where deep down we know what's best for us.

In the early years of having my own company, I stayed out of the limelight. I was the strategist, the producer, the champion of others. In part this was due to being good at it, but also because I was afraid of stepping into the light.

If we don't take risks, we can't fail, right? Wrong. Not taking any risks is the most serious failure of them all. All the other failures are learning opportunities. Never trying teaches us nothing, except that we'll never know what might have been. Choosing to remain in the smallness and perceived safety of the cage may be easier in the short term, but it steals the potential of a much richer life in the long term.

It's cramped and dark and limiting in the cage, but it's tidy. It feels safe because we know every corner of it. Outside is big and messy and bright and limitless and frankly the vast expanse of the unknown is terrifying. But that's where the light is. That's where the possibility is. That's where the fun is. That's where we can experience the joy of flight.

There is a fascinating German word *zugunruhe*, which literally translates as 'migratory restlessness'. It's the phenomenon seen in caged birds that behave in a fidgety, agitated way just before the time they would migrate, were they in the wild. We might call this 'itchy feet' or, if we want to be fancy, 'eleutheromania'.

It's an urgent sense that you need to move, a desperate craving for freedom.

Deep down we know we're not meant to be caged, but the prospect of what lies outside is scary. We peek out from between the bars to get a glimpse of a new context in the big wide world and immediately shut it off with doubt and fear: 'Who am I to do that?' 'Who am I to even want that?' 'It's too selfish.' 'It would never work.' 'What would so-and-so say?'

This is perhaps especially true for women, who are genetically designed to nurture and care for others, and often turn down opportunities under the false impression that stepping forwards would be selfish.

As Pia's story demonstrates below, we tend to do this at the cost of our own wellbeing, without realizing that in the end staying trapped doesn't serve anyone. If you limit your view to what's inside the cage, you miss the potential of all that lies beyond.

~ True self calling ~

Pia Jane Bijkerk ran a homeware boutique in Sydney, she had a boyfriend and a comfortable home, and on the surface everything looked fine. But her context made her a carer to her mother who had been seriously ill for many years, and eventually Pia began to resent the burden of duty as her untended wanderlust burned away inside.

At 28, Pia decided to break free. She made arrangements for her mother's care, put all her things in storage and moved to Paris, where she met the man she would marry and who would become the father of her child.

Pia experimented with living on a houseboat in Amsterdam, expanded her styling and photography work, and built a flexible business that worked around her family. She wrote four books, including the breathtakingly beautiful My Heart Wanders. *Most importantly she was reacquainted with her true self.*

Eventually Pia moved back to Australia to nurse her mother in the last years of her life, which she did with a deep gratitude and respect as the daughter she wanted to be.

BUILDING ESCAPE MOMENTUM

You now know what your cage looks and feels like on the inside. Now it's time to look from the outside in to start seeing things through the eyes of your free self. Getting a wider perspective on the stories you're telling yourself will help you to understand what's really going on.

Ultimately it's about seeing the difference between a life lived inside the cage and a life lived outside it, so you focus all your energy and attention on escaping into the expanse of possibility.

This is your point of departure. You are not expected to know your destination yet. Stay open. Stay alert. See where the journey takes you.

Humans are seekers by nature. There is energy and intention in the word 'seek'. It shares a root with the Latin *satire* – to perceive by scent. We have to sniff out the answers to our questions.

Seeking requires action and curiosity. We love quests, and the greatest quest of all is that of seeking freedom.

We don't need to travel to the edges of the earth to find freedom. It's right here, inside the choices that we make every day.

LOCATING YOUR FREE SELF

In that moment I lay on my bedroom floor in despair, the girl visiting me from the mountainside was my free self, reminding me that there's a big world out there. When I was on that boat at the tender age of 17, it was as if I became the expanse of the ocean, and nature was showing me how to feel free.

Your free self is always flying nearby; calling to you, trying to show you how beautiful the world is outside the cage.

Sometimes your free self comes to you as a memory or shows up as a daydream or a desire for change. Sometimes it's just a feeling, like a small child tugging at your sleeve. Your free self is ethereal, delicate and rarely shouts, so you have to get quiet, stay open and stay alert to notice what it is telling you.

You don't have to wait for your free self to show up. You can invite them in. You can imagine your free self and call them back.

Your free self is all the best bits of you, without the worries, the stress, the negative voices. The confident, brave, happy version. The curious, quirky, adventurous version. The creative, optimistic, flexible version. The version made of pure love and light. It's possible you haven't seen your free self in a while, but if you think back to the last time you felt truly free, you'll find them there.

Observing your free self activates your higher consciousness. By visualizing your free self in detail, you get drawn closer.

Entry 6: Getting to know your free self

Imagine your free self hovering outside your cage. Watch closely and ask these questions:

1. *What can your free self see?*

2. *What is making your free self feel free?*

3. *How does your free self move?*

4. *How does your free self approach life?*

5. *Who does your free self care about?*

6. *What does your free self treasure?*

7. *What is your free self trying to show you?*

8. *What does freedom mean to YOU, right now?*

The trademarks of feeling free

I asked Freedom Seekers in my community what it feels like to feel free, and without exception they described a lightness and clarity in the mind and body, a sense of wellbeing and an uplifting energy. For some people this energy was calm and gentle, for others it was vital and expansive. These are the trademarks of feeling free.

How many are familiar to you? Which sound most appealing?

In the body

- ❃ Lightness
- ❃ Relaxed
- ❃ Strong
- ❃ Energized
- ❃ Carefree
- ❃ Feel beautiful
- ❃ Physical flexibility
- ❃ Feel taller
- ❃ Heightened senses
- ❃ Zest
- ❃ Smiling
- ❃ Sense of aliveness
- ❃ Buoyant
- ❃ Healthy
- ❃ Able to breathe more deeply

In the mind

- ❃ Centred
- ❃ Open
- ❃ Content
- ❃ Joyful
- ❃ Creative
- ❃ Inspired

❀ Carefree

❀ Giddy

❀ Younger

❀ Vital

❀ Awake

❀ Empowered

❀ Inspired

❀ Safe

❀ Uncluttered

❀ Clarity

❀ Full of ideas

❀ Enthuslastlc

❀ Sunny

❀ Motivated

❀ Connected

❀ Sense of growth

❀ Expansive

❀ Focused

❀ Calm

❀ Present

❀ Confident

❀ Happy

Doesn't that all sound wonderful? Wouldn't you like to feel that way every day? Visualize how you think freedom feels, or think back to the last time you felt free, and tell yourself it won't be long until you feel that way again.

Entry 7: Birds as messengers

As you travel this path of discovery and growth, pay attention to the birds around you – in the trees, on the ground, in the skies. Imagine them as messengers from the Universe.

1. *Notice what you are doing, saying or thinking when you spot birds, alone or in groups.*

2. *Notice how they are behaving, where they are flying and how they move.*

3. *Think about what ideas and emotions their movements and behaviour spark for you.*

4. *Sketch them if you like, and jot some thoughts in your notebook. Do this every time you spot birds, and see if you notice any patterns emerging. What messages are they carrying for you?*

5. *Look out for other bird signs. Take a moment to pause when you see a feather on your path. If you see someone wearing feather jewellery or sporting a bird tattoo, consider reaching out. Ask them about it. You never know where your conversation might lead.*

Allow birds to become a symbol of possibility to inspire your flight.

Chapter 3

FREEDOM KEY 1: HEADSPACE + HEARTSPACE

It's hard to find the words to explain the impact of motherhood on my life. It is both the best and the most challenging thing I have known. The truth is, I'm not the same person that I was before children. My heart is bigger, and it grows every day. It is at much greater risk of breaking, but that's a risk worth taking.

As my heart has grown, my head has filled up with mush. Where thoughts used to be tidily filed away, there has been a break-in and everything is scattered, but there's no time to clear up the mess.

Babies do that to you. They turn you into some kind of crazy person, pumped full of love and hormones, brain cooked and memory gone. The formerly smart chick who could hold a Prime Minister in conversation finds herself scrabbling round the floor of her mind for words, reaching out to the end of the sentence she started, imploring it to come back. I have put my credit card in the fridge, gone out with my shoes on the wrong feet and walked into a room forgetting why I'm there more times than I care to remember. Fried, bamboozled, drunk on love and lack of sleep.

By the time my first baby Sienna turned six months old, I was acting like a robot. Every waking moment was spent either looking after her or working. The only 'me time' was when I took five minutes for a rushed shower, or perhaps half an hour for a hot bath – where I had a really bad habit of reading books about work.

In amongst it there were many precious moments of delight: watching her grow and explore the world, and cuddling her close. Sienna was a very happy baby who loved connecting with people and making us laugh. But I know that most of my energy was taken by simply functioning: making dinner, changing nappies, taking her for a walk and working for more hours than was healthy. Mr K (my husband) and my mum shared the load generously, looking after Sienna for large chunks of the day in between feeds, and this has led to strong bonds, which are a blessing. Grandma was Sienna's first friend and Daddy is the apple of her eye. But personally I felt like I was doing everything wrong. Not enough time. Not enough attention. Any spare thought energy going into telling myself how I was simply not enough.

I would try to feed Sienna at my computer, one moment congratulating myself for multitasking, the next cursing my aching back and berating myself for holding a baby so close to the screen. I would lie on the floor and play with her, hands in the game but my head in my inbox. At night I would be so exhausted that I couldn't sleep. Soon after I eventually dropped off, I'd be woken for another feed. My body never got the chance to recover. I know it's the same for most parents of young babies, but that knowledge doesn't make it any easier when it's your turn to go through it.

I think the worst part is that I wasn't always present. The person caring for my sweet daughter, loving her and holding her, was just a shadow of the real me. My heart was grateful but my mind was distracted, sucked out of the moments by other demands on my time. I felt powerless when I should have felt powerful, having created a small, beautiful, blue-eyed miracle.

And then came the meltdown. The moment I realized I was a caged bird, lying there on my bedroom floor, I made the decision to escape. The next thing I did was the most significant thing I could do in that state. It was the only thing I was capable of.

I decided to make a little space for myself. In order to really be with my baby, my family and my work, I first had to find my way back to myself.

In the beginning I carved out just five minutes of space, to breathe. Then 10 minutes standing barefoot in the garden, face to the sun. Then 20 minutes to make a cup of tea and read *Flow* magazine.

Soon enough it became an hour for a yoga class here, two hours for a walk on the beach there. And then I started to make space in my working practice, only dealing with one of our main projects on Tuesdays, and the other on Fridays. What surprised me most was how well this worked for others on my team too. It wasn't just me who appreciated space.

One day, when out for a walk on Hove seafront, I started fantasizing about owning one of the iconic beach huts that have stood there for years. Imagine if I had a tiny place to escape to that was all mine. A corner of quiet calm, where I could look out to sea, hear the waves and breathe slowly and deeply. Perhaps read a book. Or sketch. Or just sit. The more I thought about it, the more obsessed I became.

Beach hut 404 was covered with peeling paint and rotting, but the more I looked at it, the more I knew I wanted to rescue it. I didn't realize that in doing so I would start to rescue myself.

So I bought it. It sounds like a small thing, but even dilapidated beach huts in Hove cost a cool £12,000. But I didn't care. The money wasn't doing me much good sitting in my bank account. I'd rather be able to sit inside my savings, looking out to sea.

Soon after signing for it, I discovered the hut was so rotten I'd have to rebuild it from scratch. I also discovered that you don't actually own the land, just the hut itself, and have to rent the area beneath from the local council. So for one heart-stopping moment when we pulled it down, all that remained of my £12,000 was a pile of decaying wood. Had I actually gone insane?

In the end I built a new beach hut with the help of a talented carpenter friend. Well, he built it, and I painted it – shades of cool grey on the inside to evoke the calmness I yearned for, and candy-striped doors for some seaside cheer. I furnished it with soft cushions and a thick knitted throw for windy days. I filled its tiny bookshelf with tales of the sea, books about wave watching and island life, and faraway adventure. I filled a box with things to play with – bubbles, hand-cut stamps, a journal and a Polaroid camera – everything you might need for a day away from the world.

The beach hut was so restful that I decided to open it up to my community, so others could also find some quiet in the middle of their busy lives. The Little Beach Hut of Dreams was born. We created a programme where people could apply to use it for the day for free, to dream, plan, make art, finish their novel or just be by themselves. We had to sell The Little Beach Hut of Dreams when we moved away, but I'll always be grateful for the time she was mine.

As I slowly carved out more and more space, I saw a huge difference in myself. In the end I took a full five months of maternity leave the second time round – a long time for a business owner – and had a precious summer getting to know our new addition, baby Maia.

PAUSE, REFLECT AND BREATHE

The 'Headspace + Heartspace' Freedom Key is a way of finding room to pause, reflect and breathe. It's about finding quiet opportunities to allow your head and heart to re-attune to one another, and restore your inner calm.

The most important element of this Freedom Key is finding space – space in your day (time), space in the noise (quiet) and space in the world (place) – so you can expand the space in your heart and mind to bring clarity, serenity and calm.

By dropping into your body you can find headspace. By dropping into your sense of love, wonder and beauty, you can find heartspace.

We lead such busy lives, and most of us are constantly surrounded by noise – in our minds, in our ears, on our phones, in the world around us. This constant chatter hampers our internal signals about what we want and need, even what we love. It makes us want to shut down, instead of open up.

We are distracted at every turn. Our brains are forced to work overtime to process all the inputs. Focusing is a challenge. Our constant pursuit of more is pushing us to our limits, and the pressure is continually flooding our bodies with adrenalin, cortisol and other stress-related hormones, drawing vital resources away from our immune system and capacity to heal. No wonder so many of us are susceptible to illness, visually ageing and exhausted all the time.

Finding Headspace + Heartspace gives your brain and heart a chance to rest quietly and open gently, so the well of inspiration can be refilled.

When you open your heart and mind, you invite possibility, and make more room for love.

When you carve out the time and space to recharge, you emerge a restored version of yourself. This isn't necessarily about living quietly. It's about getting quiet, so when your life speaks it does so with strength, clarity and beauty.

This Freedom Key is helpful when everything just seems too much. When the TV makes you crazy. When you cannot hear yourself think.

When Sienna was still very small, there was a time I just wanted to turn to the kind, gentle, helpful people in my house and scream something a lot less polite than 'Will you all please just shut up?' If you know me, you'll know this is completely out of character, but in the chaos of early motherhood I was simply desperate for quiet and calm, for Headspace + Heartspace.

This Freedom Key can unlock your cage door when getting up in the morning feels like an effort, never mind getting through the day. When your mind is full and your heart is heavy. When the concept of 'feeling free' or 'doing what you love' seems a laughable fantasy, because it's all you can do to remember to eat, in between meetings and family demands and your overflowing inbox. It can be exactly what you need when you feel drained from the constant giving, emotionally supporting others at the cost of your own wellbeing.

Headspace + Heartspace will help clear the fog so you can begin to dream of flight.

Activating the Headspace + Heartspace Freedom Key

You can activate this Freedom Key by spending time in a physical place that is both restful and nurturing. Think elemental - earth, air, fire, water.

If water is a source of inspiration, find a spot on a riverbank or a bench by a lake, or take a stroll by the sea. If you need air, go high, and climb a mountain, hike up a hill, take your flask of tea to a windy clifftop. Watch the clouds or gaze at the night sky. Get up for the sunrise. Marvel at the sunset.

In Japan they have a therapy called *Shinrin-yoku*, which literally means 'forest bathing'. It invites you to drink in the healing power of the trees, to be present, grateful, aware. To walk in silence, like a fox. To explore, find quiet, sink in, open up. If you can't get to a forest, go barefoot in your garden, take your dog for a walk or explore a local park.

Nature helps, but it's not compulsory. It could be a cosy corner of your home or an armchair in your favourite cafe. It doesn't even have to be a place. It can be inside your daily run, on the pages of your journal, within a yoga pose, in the slow stirring of a risotto, in the flicker of a candle or the flames of a fire pit, on a long cycle ride, in the steam of your morning coffee.

It just has to be somewhere you can breathe deeply, unplug to reconnect. Choose wherever calls to you, and take yourself there.

If you can take yourself away somewhere for a long pause, you'll likely see a huge transformation. But even if that isn't practical right now, you can start activating this Freedom Key right where you are, with an hour here, a weekend there. Even a few minutes a day makes a difference.

At times like this it's vital to watch what you're watching, nurture yourself with gentle music and activities, and protect yourself from violent movies, sensationalist news and social media overload.

When you make space in your head and heart, and filter out any aggressive stimuli, you make room for inspiration and love to rush in.

༄

Chapter 4

FREEDOM KEY 2: ADVENTURE † ALIVENESS

Endless to-do lists, obligations and financial pressures can all make the cage bars loom closer. It's at these times that we are most likely to feel that adventure is a luxury, but this is precisely when we need to invite more adventure in.

When my business started to grow, with my team rapidly expanding and each day merging into the next with the busyness and responsibility of it all, I became something of an automaton. For too long I had felt like I was going through the motions: observing life without being inside it, living the experience. So I challenged myself with small adventures. Daring myself to go somewhere new here, talking to a stranger there. With every small step, I felt more alive. And not only that, I returned to my business with fresh ideas, more energy and heightened creativity.

Mr K could see it happening, so he suggested I visit somewhere new for a real break from my day-to-day life. My old friend Vigdis had moved to Costa Rica a decade or so ago, to set up a kayak lodge, and I had always wanted to visit her so it seemed like the perfect opportunity. I was hesitant at first, as Maia would be just 10 months old, but I booked it anyway. When the time came to actually go, she voluntarily stopped breastfeeding a couple of days beforehand, as if she too were giving me her blessing.

Kayaking with Vigdis in Costa Rica, I am shooting silver sparks from the ends of my fingers. Flick, flick, I feel like a superhero. As I splash my oar on the surface of the inky water, I make diamonds scatter across a watery ballroom floor.

If I hold my oar vertically and pull it up through the blackness, a white witchy woman rises from below with hair floating around her head, some goddess of the deep. I am on a night kayak tour paddling amidst bioluminescence in a secret bay in the tropics. The sky is quiet and the air is warm. In the shadow of a tiny island, headlamp switched off, it is coal black and eerily silent. I am enchanted.

I look at Vigdis, a dark shadow gliding stealthily past. A rare moonbeam catches her face and she is radiant. 'Isn't it amazing?' she says, her golden hair glowing. Vigdis has seen this phenomenon hundreds of times, yet her sense of awe never wanes. This is her job, and I am staying with her to find out how she escaped her cage and left her home country of Norway to end up here, running a kayak and sport fishing lodge in Paquera.

I have known Vigdis for 12 years, but the details of her life have been a casualty of the busyness of everyday life. Seeing her again, I discover a happily married Freedom Seeker who has created exactly the life she wants, living among exotic animals and birds, working from a treehouse and spending every day in nature with her husband by her side.

∼ Making freedom happen ∼

Vigdis Vatshaug and her husband Thomas Jones had good jobs back in Norway, but they longed for adventure and dreamed of a place in the trees, near a beach where they could fish and kayak and share that experience with fellow adventurers. And so began a search which took them to Costa Rica.

Although they made a bold move by relocating there, they are not high-rolling risk-takers. They made a checklist of what was important to them: an abundance of nature, water activities, a politically stable country, relative safety for travellers, accessibility from Europe and the US and so on. Determined to learn Spanish, they ruled out any English-speaking countries and focused on Central America. They reached out to contacts for advice, and invested in a six-week scouting trip to find the right place. It was a heady time and when they finally found this spot near Paquera, they knew their search was over.

Now Vigdis and Thomas welcome their guests in a huge open living room, the wooden roof held up by whole trunks of frangipani trees. There are no walls here, no inside and outside. Pink and white bougainvillea spills into the breakfast area, and when the rain comes the atmosphere is electric. From a swing seat in the lounge you can see down to the crystal water and pristine white sand, silhouetted hammocks swinging gently in the breeze.

Guests often remark on their lifestyle, some clearly thinking they are crazy, others with a tinge of jealousy. 'You're so lucky,' they say. But it's not about luck. Vigdis and Thomas made this happen. They chose to make certain sacrifices, which others might not be prepared to make, in order to create the life they wanted.

They have had their share of challenges along the way, but they have supported each other through it all, keeping their eyes on the prize.

Vigdis is a Freedom Seeker who escaped her cage using the Freedom Key of Adventure + Aliveness. She changed everything about her life, moved continents, learned a new language and created a whole new career so she could sense that adventure and aliveness every day. And as long as she does that, she stays clear of the cage and flies free.

Back in the kayaks Vigdis and I are laughing, firing sparks at each other. We decide she is Bio Woman and I am Lumio. We joke, but Vigdis really does have the superpower of shining a light of inspiration just by the way she lives.

CHALLENGING YOURSELF

The Freedom Key of 'Adventure + Aliveness' is a way to jolt you out of the monotony of the everyday. It's about challenging yourself with something new, different and unpredictable. It's a fizz of excitement, and a break from the old routine.

Adventure is a mindset. It's about seeking out the unknown in all parts of your life. It's a thirst for freshness. It's an active pursuit of inspiration. It's the thrill of pushing yourself in new territory.

Adventure often involves risk, and even sometimes danger. The gift of this is the acute focus required, which obliterates the demands of the normal world in the moment.

Aliveness is about being in the moment, drinking it all in. It's about noticing and appreciating, and basking in your own sense of wonder. It's about allowing yourself to be in awe.

This Freedom Key is about realizing you are part of something bigger than yourself, part of a fascinating and mysterious wider world. It's about wanting to witness it first-hand and taking action to make that happen.

What is the opposite of adventure – boredom and monotony perhaps? And the opposite of aliveness doesn't even bear thinking about. That's why this Freedom Key is so important. It's about the beating heart of life itself. It's about engaging with the world around you, being an explorer and a collector of moments. It's about so much of what can make living in this world so exciting.

BECOMING MORE AWARE

Earlier in my career I worked for the UN, and had to undertake security training before going overseas. Besides teaching us how to avoid being kidnapped and stepping on landmines, the course taught us that routines are dangerous. Imagine a diplomat taking the same journey to work each day, in the same vehicle, along the same roads, at the same time. To do so would be to invite an ambush. It is actually safer to change things up regularly and add an element of surprise.

This type of awareness can also benefit our lives. We tend to slip into routines, as they somehow feel easier and safer; but they are actually quietly dangerous. Routines can make us feel good because they make us feel busy, something that many of us wear as a badge of honour. But busyness does not equate to usefulness. Motion does not equate to progress.

Professional adventurer and author of *Microadventures* and *Grand Adventures* Alastair Humphreys told me,

> *'Physical adventure is a powerful way to lift yourself out of the daily grind because it involves primal things like being tired, or cold, or scared. That doesn't happen much in our sanitized lives. Doing difficult things in big, wild landscapes helps us reset our sense of perspective.'*

Adventure + Aliveness is also important because it is so effective for problem solving. Use it to tackle your challenges in new ways and see them as opportunities to do things differently. An adventurous spirit will take you outside of your problems, pull you over obstacles, usher you up hills and show you the beauty of what lies beyond.

Freedom is our essence, and we feel most connected to that essence when we come alive.

The Adventure + Aliveness Freedom Key is most powerful when you need lifting out of the drudgery of yet another day like yesterday. When you feel a bit jaded, when your faith is waning and you find yourself miserable or moody. When life has become predictable and you're bored, left wondering, 'Is this all there is?'

It's also surprisingly useful when you feel like you just can't fit one more thing into your day, because it can be part of your day just by switching up the way you do the things you need to do.

On a larger scale, it's a crucial Freedom Key when you find yourself at a crossroads, with the opportunity for a major change but little idea of which direction to take. Why? It can open your eyes to vast possibility, and help you recognize your own potential.

Just think how different you are, when you become the most adventurous and alive version of yourself.

Activating the Adventure + Aliveness Freedom Key

Adventure + Aliveness doesn't have to mean moving to the other side of the planet, living in a jungle or dropping everything to go on a round-the-world trip. It just asks you to try new things or do things differently.

Adventure doesn't have to cost much and you can activate this Freedom Key in simple ways, perhaps by dropping a pin on a map and going there, ditching your routine or doing something spontaneous.

Even if your current situation requires you to be in one place, be a traveller in spirit and see where it takes you. When we are on the road we sample new foods, try out new words, use different modes of transport, stay up all night counting the shooting stars. Try it at home. Walk around your town imagining everyone has a story and everything is interesting. Go to a new restaurant, close your eyes and pick something at random from the menu. Talk to strangers. Sit awhile and people watch.

Mix it up and taste the difference. It'll put your senses on high alert, and plunge you deep into the moment, soaking up the glory of life.

Chapter 5

FREEDOM KEY 3: PLAYFULNESS + CURIOSITY

Once I'd made the decision to escape the cage, my senses were on high alert, and what I noticed really surprised me. There was a distinct absence of the sound of laughter. Not a complete absence, but laughing to the point of losing all sense of normality had become a rare occurrence. For someone who loves to laugh, that was sad indeed. As I thought about this, I recalled I a time when my natural sense of playfulness and curiosity had led me somewhere I'll never forget.

❧

I was accompanying the actor James Nesbitt, a UNICEF Ambassador, on a visit to some development projects in Zambia. He was with a television crew inside a tiny, breezeblock house talking with a young family and there wasn't enough room for all of us, so I snuck off for a wander around the community.

I came to a dusty clearing surrounded by more tiny dwellings. It was deserted. I saw a stick on the ground and felt strangely drawn to it, so I picked it up. It was as if that stick had magic powers. Suddenly I found myself skipping along, swinging my arms to and fro while holding the stick like some kind of wand. And then I heard the padding of bare feet in the dust.

A young boy was following me. His shaved head was bouncing rhythmically, as he too skipped, and he burst out laughing. Within seconds he was joined by a couple of friends. Within minutes I was skipping around the clearing like the Pied Piper, with more than 50 children jostling behind me giggling and flashing delighted grins. It was astonishing.

I got curious about how far I could push it. I changed the game. I crouched down low and moved slowly, like I was stalking a lion. I put my finger to my lips and shushed them all. Instant silence, although you could tell they were desperate to laugh. We all crouched and stalked, this way and that, until I stopped, turned and roared. They fell about laughing and signalled for me to do it again. Round and round we went, stalking and roaring and cheering. We didn't speak each other's languages, but we were completely in sync. Photographer Francois D'Elbee, who had joined us on the trip and was also exploring the community, quietly captured one of the 'sshhhh' moments, and you can see a sparkle in the eyes of every single one of us. We were deep in the moment, drinking in a heady cocktail of playful curiosity and pure joy.

During my time at UNICEF I went on 17 field visits, travelled the world and met some extraordinary people, from Nobel Peace Prize winners to global leaders, from campaigning celebrities to brave community activists, and so many children facing challenging futures. But of all of the moments it's this one, in a dusty clearing in Zambia, that will forever be in my heart.

At the end of the day all we have is the sum of the precious moments we hold close, and so many of them are born from a place of playfulness and curiosity.

EXPLORE THE WORLD LIKE A CHILD

That flashback to Zambia reminded me how easy it is to experience joy, especially with children in my life. From that day onward, I made a conscious effort to be more playful and light-hearted in the way I went about things, with my baby girls as my teachers.

I also made a conscious effort to be curious about the world around me once more, wandering and exploring without an actual point or destination. Often we try to cram so much into our days that anything without an obvious goal gets jettisoned. But those moments of 'point-less' curiosity are often when we discover something that sparks an idea, opens our minds or invites a new opportunity.

The Playfulness + Curiosity Freedom Key invites you to explore the world like a child. To lighten up and not take things quite so seriously. It appeals to your inquisitiveness. It's a way of learning and discovering things about the world, without it feeling like hard work. There's a cheekiness, an innocence and an openness in it. It encourages you to loosen up and find delight. And the best thing about it? It's really easy.

When you feel light and carefree, when you have fun and laugh from deep in your belly, everything is released. Through play we connect to joy, raise our mood, practise socializing and connect to others. It's good for your body and good for your mind. Even science tells us so. There is a growing body of evidence (brilliantly summarized in Stuart Brown's book, *Play*) to show that people come up with much better creative solutions when they are playful in their approach, and not attached to the outcome.

Play demands all your attention, so your mind is free from worry. As the past and future vanish, so do your cage bars.

Being inquisitive is also vital to expanding your sense of the world: the more you discover, the more you realize there is to discover, and with that comes a sense of excitement and possibility. So have fun with it!

Play can also give us an important sense of belonging, so Playfulness + Curiosity can help us seek out those places to belong.

~ **Master of play** ~

After several years of living rough, Kevin Carroll was abandoned by his mother in a trailer park aged six, and sent to live with his grandparents. Nearby was a playground and that's where he learned and thrived.

Kevin went on to become Head Athletic Trainer for NBA team the Philadelphia 76ers, and then to work at Nike, where he frequently used playfulness and curiosity to spark huge breakthroughs in the company's work. Now he is an author, speaker and powerful agent for social change, with play being the enduring thread through it all.

For over 30 years Kevin has taken time once a week to look up, change his perspective, and journal whatever he sees. It has allowed him to look at things differently in all aspects of his life, and forever have the curious eyes of a child. Why not try it yourself?

BE MORE CURIOUS

Sometimes, it's fun to do something random, just because…

Some years back I was lamenting the decline in handwritten letters, moaning to my younger brother, Matt, about how everything arriving in the post lately seemed to be bills and advertisements. We decided to do something about it, by sending things to each other, just for fun. And so began the Campaign for Real Mail.

We challenged ourselves to put stamps on random objects, no envelopes allowed, to see what would actually arrive. Successfully delivered items included a slice of toast, a pair of sunglasses, a CD, a pineapple and a tin of sardines. Then Matt sent me an empty lavatory roll. Except, when it arrived, it wasn't empty.

The cardboard tube was delivered with a newspaper rolled up in it. And not any old local newspaper, but *The Arnold Sentinel* from Custer County, Arnold, Nebraska, USA, 4,400 miles away. We had absolutely no idea how it got into the lavatory roll. This sparked my curiosity.

I started to read the newspaper and got an unexpected insight into life in Custer County. There was a story about a deer caught in a snowstorm and an announcement that the 'Good News Club' would resume soon. I liked the sound of that. I sent an email to the newspaper to share this mystery, and they published an article about it, piquing the curiosity of their readers too. It made me smile.

There was no financial reward or end goal for this exercise. We were simply curious about where it might go. Sometimes that's reason enough. Sometimes it leads somewhere you would never have expected.

Playfulness + Curiosity is the perfect Freedom Key to activate when you feel like life has become too serious. When you find yourself hunched over your computer at all hours, when you aren't challenged at work or when your head is full of worry.

And if you think there isn't time for fun, this is definitely the one for you, right now.

Activating the Playfulness + Curiosity Freedom Key

I have two experts on play living in my house. Their names are Sienna and Maia, and they do little else all day long. Here's a quick rundown of their average day: Wake up, smile, eat, play, get dressed, chat, play, smile, watch *Peppa Pig*, play some more, laugh, chat, make me laugh, dance, explore, hunt for snails, jump on the sofa, draw, blow bubbles, giggle, eat, tickle, wander round the house wearing a tutu and tiara, throw a ball around (still wearing the tutu and tiara), eat, put on pyjamas, sing, read a book, try to negotiate more time to play, fall asleep, repeat.

My eldest daughter learns nearly everything through Playfulness + Curiosity. It's how she grasps and assimilates what's around her. It's how she makes friends, and how she involves her baby sister, and us, in her world. Terrible Twos aside, she is in a happy mood nearly all the time. There has to be something to learn from that. Imagine what might happen if you got more curious, and started being more playful.

Think about what you used to love to do as a child, and see how you can integrate any aspect of that into your daily life now. If your work environment is not conducive to play, being playful can feel wonderfully subversive. If you don't work right now, how much more playful could you be in carrying out your daily tasks?

What about curiosity? Think about the last time you picked up an unfamiliar magazine, went on a treasure hunt, investigated something that puzzled you. Follow your curiosity and see where it leads.

Chapter 6

FREEDOM KEY 4: CREATIVITY + INNOVATION

The more I made space in my life, the more I noticed, and the more I felt drawn to record the latter part of my pregnancy and the precious early days of Maia's life. I started to journal my experience, tracking the beauty and the wonder, along with the challenges of understanding the new shape of our little family. The more I wrote, the more I recognized my own context and cage, and the more clearly I could see the door and the world beyond it. The time I spent writing opened up more and more space, in my head and in my heart. My Freedom Keys were feeding each other and I was writing myself free.

The more I prioritized the writing, the more I realized how important it was to me. And as I created more and more space, something special slipped in to fill the expanse – a big idea about personal freedom. This gave me even more reason to keep creating, exploring concepts and possibilities. It brought me such joy I started to think of ways to innovate my life and business to allow for more space, more writing, and more freedom.

It wasn't the first time that creativity had been the catalyst for escape, and for innovating my career. Some seven years earlier, the simple act of going on an art retreat changed the trajectory of my life.

$$\sim$$

The seatbelt sign is on and the air stewardess is demonstrating how to use the life jackets in case of emergency. I'm heading to California for an art retreat where I don't know a soul. I have a to-do list as long as my arm, more work deadlines than I care to think about, and I don't have time for this. I don't even paint. What on earth am I doing hopping on a transatlantic flight?

Rewind a few weeks and I am lying in bed reading a book by an American mixed media artist called Kelly Rae Roberts, *Taking Flight*. It's a painting manual, but more than that it's a gentle guide to embracing your creative self. There's something in this woman's story that calls to me, so I fire up my computer and look her up. On her website it says she's co-teaching a workshop in San Jose in a few weeks' time, with artist Mati Rose McDonough. I have no idea where San Jose is, but I book a place on the workshop… And then discover San Jose is 5,000 miles away, on the west coast of the USA.

When I arrive, all I want to do is turn around and get on the next plane home. Everyone seems to know each other, and they unload the kind of art supplies that makes it clear they are artists already. Whatever was I thinking? What right do I have to be here? Who do I think I am?

But my taxi has already driven off, so I might as well stay. Little do I know it will turn out to be one of the most important experiences of my life.

We gathered to paint, and there in the shadow of a redwood forest on ancient tribal land, we unfurled, explored, connected. I was happy from the first wisps of morning until the last breath of night.

As a child I was always keen to show new dances or plays I had made up to anyone who would watch. I spent hours developing negatives in the photography darkroom my dad built in our garage, and I loved to get messy with paint as most children do. But as I grew older, doubts began to set in: I had no formal art education, no technique training, no idea about what I 'should' be doing. Who was I to put art out in the world? Surely everyone would think I was an unqualified fraud? I became increasingly shy about showing my creativity in any form. In fact, for years most of my friends had no idea I even liked making things.

The art world always seemed to be this mysterious, impenetrable clique of incredibly talented people, accessible only with an MA in Fine Art, several gallery exhibitions under your belt and a little black book of art dealers' contact details. I didn't have any of those so I slowly drifted away, not just from painting, but also photography, writing and all other creative pursuits. When creative confidence goes it doesn't just seep away, it drains right out.

That was until I went on that art retreat in 2010. It drew me back and everything changed. There I met a group of women who were just like me. But these women weren't hiding their creativity – they were embracing and celebrating it. There was support instead of competition and genuine encouragement where judgement used to be.

I felt so lucky to have discovered this tribe, tightly bound by a shared passion for creativity, a curiosity to learn and a love of life. It was a rare opportunity to indulge in the luxury of a four-day creative adventure under the supporting guidance of inspirational artists, in the company of some very special souls. Safe in the knowledge that there were no mistakes, we happily painted, laughed and told stories into the early hours. It was absolute bliss.

Although everyone came to the retreat at a different stage of their artistic career – some full-time professional artists, some art teachers, some just starting out – we all, in our own way, unfurled our wings, dusted them down and prepared to take flight. And in the years since I have seen so many of those women really soar in their creative lives. They have innovated their own way of living, changed careers, run retreats, moved continents, become teachers, written books, and stayed friends.

Magic happened on that Native American land, and none of us were quite the same again.

For my part this creative awakening was a huge turning point in my life. It was the catalyst for me creating a business that would go on to encourage thousands of women to walk their own creative paths. It would be a doorway to innovating everything about the way I made a living, and helping others innovate their own lives.

In time, Kelly Rae Roberts would became a business partner and friend, and tarot readers would tell me we were sisters in a former life. Who'd have thought all that could come from a book and a paintbrush?

Creativity and innovation are means to an end. And sometimes an end in themselves. For many of us, they are also a beginning.

THE MAGIC OF CREATIVITY

The Freedom Key of Creativity + Innovation is about experimentation, invention and reinvention. Thinking differently and making differently. It's about doing the unexpected or the unusual. It's both a behaviour and an attitude. And often it's art too. We are all unique beings and creativity is our way of expressing it, while innovation is our way of applying that uniqueness to challenges in the world.

Creativity has a special kind of power. Once you let it in, it can take you places you could never have imagined. It doesn't care if you're 'good' at it. It just wants to be welcomed. The truth is I struggled for a long time to recognize myself as a creative person, but that's ridiculous because to be human is to be creative. We just need to find the right outlet for each of us and then let it in.

Creativity is imagination at work – it's the most soulful way we can express our deepest selves, and embrace beauty and possibility. It's the realization of something that didn't exist in a particular form before you made it that way. It's proactive: making things and making things happen.

As a Freedom Key, when you are trying to get out of the cage, the point is not the product, it's the process; it's not the created, it's the creating. It's not the innovated, it's the innovating. And that means there are no mistakes. So you have nothing to lose by trying.

Personal growth is the constant innovation and re-creation of our own lives. If nothing has worked for you so far, then you'd better try something else.

CREATIVE THERAPY

Through our online courses I have seen how creativity can lift people out of the fog of chronic illness, help them cope with loss and recover from broken relationships. I have seen some people express themselves on a canvas in a way they couldn't in words, and others discover who they are in the ink of a pen.

Being creative is often a large part of doing what you love, as a route to feeling free. That doesn't necessarily just mean being creative with your hands, but also with your mind – how you approach your situation, your options, your opportunities. It might mean taking more photos, making more art or doing more journaling, but it also might mean asking more questions, making different choices, tackling old problems in a new way.

Talking about creativity – and expressing it in whatever form – can make you feel awkward and vulnerable. Many of us are afraid of showing our paintings, reading aloud what we have written, playing music we have created in front of others, talking about our ideas or sharing our dreams. We often think we are not good enough and are scared to reveal what has come from deep within us. But when we do, we step closer to living as our true selves, a crucial part of what it means to feel free.

The Freedom Key of Creativity + Innovation can help when you feel uninspired, in need of beauty and interest in your life. If you can just take that first step, doing one creative thing, or innovating one part of your life, you will expose yourself to a virtuous cycle of inspiration and expression.

Creativity and innovation are not born from nothing. We need inspiration in, to get ideas out. We have to seek out inspiration, and then it becomes a virtuous cycle. The more we allow ourselves to be creative and innovative, the more we open up the channel for that inspiration to flow.

When you are struggling in the shadows of your cage bars, especially when they involve emotions such as despair, anger and frustration, this Freedom Key can help. Using these triggers as catalysts, instead of allowing them to eat you up inside, can be a recipe for explosive creativity and brilliant innovation. Often, in doing this, you will invite new doors of opportunity to swing open.

It's almost impossible to simultaneously be 'in the zone' and worry about daily life. And often, while you're busy creating or innovating something, your subconscious gets busy solving whatever problem you had been worrying about.

It's worth noting that creativity can unearth deeply buried issues and challenges, so you may want to consider getting creative in a supported space, with a teacher you trust or a group of friends.

FLOCKING TOGETHER

African legends tell of bird migrations bringing fertility to the land; similarly, flocks of like minded Freedom Seekers can fertilize ideas and make things happen. Two of our online creative course portfolios, www.makeartthatsells.com with Lilla Rogers and www.makeitindesign.com with Rachael Taylor are well known for their amazing class communities, which connect like-minded people from across the world. Both sets of courses have seen artists and designers bond so closely that they have gone on to form professional collectives, pooling knowledge and resources to exhibit together at top international trade shows, and grow their careers together.

Stronger together

Emma McGowan, a copywriter by trade, is now building a freelance business as a surface pattern designer. Having graduated from several of our courses, Emma is part of the Four Corners Art Collective that met through their online studies, and a number of the group have exhibited together at the Surtex Trade Show in New York.

Having flocked together around a shared passion, these talented artists and designers are helping each other rise up. Rather than competing for clients, they have seen they are stronger together, offering a diverse collection of work, different strengths, and crucially the moral support that is so vital for professional creatives. And that support has been crucial for Emma, as having 'colleagues' to check in with, who get it and are rooting for you, makes all the difference.

Activating the Creativity + Innovation Freedom Key

If you're under the impression that there are two types of people, 'creative' and 'not creative', I assure you that is a myth. We all have creative capacities, but some people use them more than others. It is possible to develop these creative capacities over time - sometimes this happens through need and sometimes through desire - and with practice, we naturally become more in tune with our creativity. Don't be fooled into thinking it has to be learned. It doesn't. Technique, yes. But creativity is in you already. All you need to do is to feed your creative soul. And innovation stems from creative thinking, so if you can be creative, you can be innovative.

For most of us, our creative journey began earlier than we realize, and runs deeper than we know. Along the way, we discover new mediums of expression and new parts of ourselves. This Freedom Key is about the way that you interpret the world, and what you do with that information. Discovering and pursuing what you want to do and be and feel in your life is one of the greatest creative adventures you could ever undertake.

Write something. Make something. Build something. Anything. Just do something creative. Don't judge the outcome, just start the process.

If you're stuck, you might like to try one of the following right now:

- Decorate the cover of your journal. Use any media you like. Write the word 'freedom' in fancy lettering.

- Write a poem about feeling free.

- Go for a walk and take photos of things that inspire you then stick them in your journal with a few notes about each one.

- Pick a colour and search for it everywhere you go today. Document what you find.

- Beautify a room in your home.

- Arrange some flowers and put them on your desk.

- Paint some stones.

- Sign up for a creative online class.

- Go to an art shop and choose a few things to experiment with. Gather up a load of natural items, like sticks, seedpods and leaves, or waste items like an old toothbrush, or a pen that no longer works, then dip them in ink or paint, and make marks on a page. Turn some music up loud and dance while you do it. Remember, don't judge the outcome, just enjoy the process.

- Make someone a card and send it.

Now you have got the creative juices flowing, think of a problem you have been grappling with at home or at work. Write down everything you assume to be true about that problem. Now write the reverse, and imagine that it's actually the reverse that is true. See if this sparks a new kind of solution to the problem. This kind of creative thinking is the partner of innovation, and can help you find new ways to tackle the challenges in your everyday life.

Chapter 7

FREEDOM KEY 5: BOLDNESS + BRAVERY

Over time my big idea about freedom became a book proposal, which brought with it a new kind of excitement. What if it actually made a difference to people? What if my ideas could actually set others free?

Hot on the tails of that hope came doubts and fears. Who am I to even think of writing a book? What makes my ideas different? Why should anyone read what I have to say?

My inner critic and inner sage went back and forth relentlessly.

I knew I could surrender to my inner critic and my pages would never see the light of day. But I also knew that if I summoned courage and chose to make my inner sage the champion, magic might just happen. Boldness + Bravery was the order of the day: boldness to make the choice to submit my book proposal and bravery to go ahead and do it. I just needed a reminder that I had done brave things before. I recalled something that happened in Japan soon after leaving university, when I was younger and less worried about the outcome. It reminded me how brave I can be.

Every minute of every day, the ego and soul are doing battle. When courage is absent, the ego keeps on winning. But when courage is present, the soul wins, every time.

The Director bowed and gestured for me to take a seat on the low black leather sofa.

'Do you like noodles?' he asked, as if that's how conversations with strangers always begin.

'Sure,' I replied. Well actually I said, 'There is really no need for you to extend such a beneficent kindness down to my humble self, but I respectfully admit that I do have something of a liking for most honourable soba.'

The man was the head of the Yamagata Cable Television Station, and after half an hour of cold noodles and small talk about apples, apple jelly and a local hot spring filled with apples to make your skin soft (Yamagata is famous for apples), I walked out with my own TV show. In Japanese. With my name in the title. Oh boy!

I remember getting on my rickety silver bicycle, throwing my handbag in the basket and heading off up the hill, looking back over my shoulder and shaking my head at what had just happened. At the time I was on the JET Programme, working as a Coordinator for International Relations for the Yamagata Prefectural Government, in a remote snowy place in northern Japan – fresh out of university, clutching a degree in Japanese and up for adventure.

Most days consisted of translating letters between government officials and their counterparts in our sister cities in the US and Indonesia, attending cultural festivals, teaching children about my country and interpreting for any visiting dignitaries. For the record, the Governor of Colorado excelled at karaoke. I even got to be the Chief of Police for a day. But this TV show was something else.

A week prior to the noodle encounter, my supervisor had asked me if there was anything I'd really like to do while in Yamagata. I guessed snowboarding in government time was out of the question, so I said, half-joking, 'It would be fun to be on the radio.'

'Eetou... Anou... Saa...' he puffed, looking away. This is the Japanese equivalent of, 'Hmm... Well... Actually I'm really sorry but that isn't going to be possible, but I don't want to lose face by telling you so...'

But then he had an idea. 'I have an acquaintance...' he started, which was usually an indication that something interesting was going to happen. 'I'll see if I can set up a meeting.'

A week later I was summoned to the cable TV station to meet the head honcho, with no idea of what was in store. In Japan, it's a serious faux pas to back out of something when someone has gone to the trouble of arranging it for you so I had to go. I was terrified and thrilled in equal measure. Was I going to get a few seconds on the local news? That would be fun.

Of course I would shortly discover that I had a year-long contract for a regular programme with my name on it. And the first thing they said was, 'We need some foreigners for the opening credits.' So I threw a big party, invited all my friends in fancy dress and got far too drunk. Even then it wasn't really real, until they shoved a huge microphone in my face and told me to introduce the show.

As it turns out, my Japanese is better when I'm slightly inebriated, and my stint in television ended up being some of the most fun I had in that snowy town. In time I managed to present without drinking a swift beer first. I even got recognized by a monk in a temple 1,000 steps up the side of a mountain, but then, as I was probably the only foreigner for 100 miles with peroxide blonde hair, it isn't really saying that much.

The point is, thinking back to that TV show, which thankfully aired pre-YouTube, I reminded myself that I could do brave things. When I couldn't bear the thought of putting myself out there, I reminded myself that I presented an entire television series, in Japanese for goodness sake, so if I could do that I can do anything.

And it's the same for you. You will have that story somewhere in your history. Take a moment to think about a time that you surprised yourself just how bold and brave you can be.

What looks brave to others may not feel brave to you, which is often why we think other people are braver than us. The truth is we are all bolder than we think, and braver than we know.

MAKING CHOICES

At its heart, the Freedom Key of Boldness + Bravery is all about making choices. Choosing to do the hard thing, the scary thing, the unknown thing, the thing you failed at before, the thing someone told you that you couldn't do, the thing you have told yourself you cannot do. It's about taking action in the direction of the very thing that makes you afraid.

If we stay safe and small, never pushing ourselves, our life never expands beyond the bars of the cage. We feel stuck, stifled and stressed. Being trapped serves no one, least of all ourselves.

To live fully we have to make ourselves bigger, to step forth and burst through the bars. Sometimes we do that with small steps, sometimes we do it in great leaps.

EASE YOURSELF IN

Some years ago I found myself at an open-air spa. It was February, and the snow was high. It was -6°C outside, so you can understand my shock at discovering you had to go in naked. I jumped in as fast as I could, delighting in the heat that penetrated my body.

I sat awhile looking out at a snowy mountain in the distance. After a few minutes I slowly raised a toe out of the water and put it back in. The feeling of bitter cold followed by nurturing heat was delicious. So then I put my foot out, up to my ankle, and back in, 'Mmmm.' Then my whole leg, 'Wow, that's cold,' but heavenly when it was back in the hot water.

And so it went on until I eventually lifted my whole self out of the hot tub and rolled in the snow, laughing. When I came to my senses I jumped back in and spent 20 minutes in a higher state of bliss, watching the sun set over the mountains.

If someone had told me to go and roll in the snow as soon as I'd arrived I would have thought they were mad, and probably not done it. If I had just got into the hot tub and never tried getting out and then back in, I wouldn't have experienced that level of bliss. This is exactly how it works with our comfort zone. Each time we stretch it, it becomes a little bigger, and we become confident that we are capable of a little more. Or a lot more.

Gently try something new, then something bigger, and before you know it you'll be rolling naked in the snow and basking in your new level of bravery. What seemed hard before suddenly makes you happy. Just think, what could be waiting for you just beyond your comfort zone?

⁓ Team See Possibilities ⁓

My friend Alison Qualter Berna discovered this for herself when she turned 40. Alison was married with three gorgeous children, a beautiful home and a thriving business. With her husband Bobby and closest friends, she had co-founded 'Apple Seeds' when her twin girls were small, to provide nurturing indoor play spaces for children in New York City. Alison loved her job, but she also wanted something outside of work and family that was just for her. She felt she had lost her sense of adventure, and wanted to reclaim it.

Restless, Alison scribbled down a bucket list of ideas on the night of her milestone birthday. That list morphed into a personal challenge to undertake one great big adventure every year. The adventure had to be physically demanding, new and inspiring.

She eased herself in with 15 yoga classes in five days, which she undertook with her friend Charles Scott. They then competed in a half ironman, before doing the Grand Canyon 'Rim to Rim to Rim' challenge, which involves running 46 miles with nearly 7,000 metres of elevation change, over rugged terrain on narrow trails.

In the half ironman, Alison met Dan Berlin and Brad Graff, who agreed to join the Grand Canyon challenge. If the run itself wasn't difficult enough, Dan was registered blind, having lost his sight in his thirties due to cone-rod dystrophy.

Dan became a huge inspiration to Alison, and together the four of them became Team See Possibilities, pushing each other far beyond their comfort zones and bonding in the process. After the Grand Canyon, she and the team led Dan to become the first *blind athlete to conquer the entire Inca Trail to Machu Picchu in one day.*

What began as a vague idea scribbled on a notepad in the dark became a way to connect with kindred spirits and become part of something bigger, which has raised many thousands of dollars for charity and inspired others – not least her own children – to see what is possible.

Activating the Freedom Key of Boldness + Bravery can help you when you need to make a practical change or take a different direction. When a decision or action feels right but seems too big for you, this Freedom Key can be the boost you need to get it done. It can give voice to your inner knowing, and wings to your dreams.

It may seem counterintuitive, but activating this Freedom Key when you're lacking confidence is the fastest way to get it back. If things are difficult anyway, you have very little to lose and everything to gain.

What if you fail? Yes, but what if you succeed?

Activating the Boldness + Bravery Freedom Key

Boldness + Bravery show themselves in many guises. Sometimes they are in-your-face big decisions, leaps of faith that put your heart in your mouth and get the adrenalin pumping. But sometimes they are gentle in the way they show up, encouraging you to take the longer road, make the more difficult choice or simply to trust. And when you do that, magic happens.

Making a conscious decision to be bold and brave can be all you need to take a chance. It is easiest to use this Freedom Key when you're buoyed up and confident, but it is most important to use it when you feel small, with limited options and a lack of hope.

Having the courage to say yes to that first date is the first step to having the courage to say yes to that marriage proposal. Having the courage to ask for respect could be an important step towards having the courage to submit those divorce papers and start over. Having the courage to set boundaries could be the first step to a healthier working arrangement. Having the courage to start that conversation could open up space for a new opportunity.

Being bold and brave in all of the parts of our lives, even when it doesn't really matter, can help us to be bold and brave when it really does.

Sometimes choosing to do nothing *yet* is a smart move. You give yourself time to gather more intelligence. To scope it out. To tune in to your gut. But 'yet' isn't an excuse. Choosing to 'do nothing yet' is very different from choosing to 'do nothing'.

On the other side of choosing to do nothing lies boredom, complacency, guilt, stuckness, regret.

On the other side of choosing to do something that takes boldness and bravery await excitement, pride and immense possibility.

Which will you choose?

Chapter 8

FREEDOM KEY 6: CONNECTION + COMMUNICATION

With my first pregnancy I joined the National Childbirth Trust (NCT) and Mr K and I attended weekly preparing-for-birth sessions with the soon-to-be-parents of other children who would be born around the same time as Sienna. At our first meeting the group leader asked what we were afraid of with regards to becoming parents. Knowing we were expecting a girl, Mr K answered, 'Boys.' Clearly he was thinking pretty far ahead. It made everyone laugh, and a bond was struck between us all.

When the class ended us mothers-to-be met up several times before our babies arrived, sympathizing about our collective bulk, our aches and pains, our trepidation about all that lay ahead. And we would share in the excitement on the eve of becoming mothers, knowing that life as we knew it was about to change forever. In the space of six weeks all our babies had been welcomed into the world and we had shifted, never to return.

Most of the women had a year's maternity leave. I had about four days. Seriously. On the fifth day after Sienna's birth, I was typing an email, head still fuzzy from the drugs, brain foggy from the utter exhaustion, but my to-do list pulling at my sleeve reminding me I had committed to something in January. Sienna was two weeks 'late', so January was nearly here, and suddenly everything was rushing headlong at me. I wonder now if that's the moment my free self upped and left. She saw me sink into a muffled greyness, feeling my way through each day, torn and shredded, loved up and smashed down. The extremes of emotion, the full heart, the empty energy reserves.

The further I went under, the more I retreated from other people, even my NCT friends. I remember a day we met up at the local cinema for a special screening for parents with their babies. It had taken me over an hour to get out the door, so just getting there felt like a major achievement. Afterwards we went to a local cafe for tea. I was a happy new mother, out with her adorable baby, and new mum pals. Everything was perfect for a moment.

But then Sienna woke up, and the crying began. I picked her up to cuddle her, offered her milk, changed her nappy, walked her round, jiggled her, talked to her, everything I could think of, but nothing worked. I was trying to talk to the other mothers, conscious that my tiny baby was screaming the place down and disturbing everyone else, and I had absolutely no idea what to do about it. I wanted to look like I was this cool, calm mother who still went to the cinema and drank tea and chatted to friends while her baby cooed on her lap. Instead I was embarrassed, frustrated and upset that I didn't have a clue what to do.

In the end I made my excuses and left. I ran the whole way home, hoping I might find the answer there, pushing my pram and crying about how I couldn't make my baby happy or hold a conversation or talk to the others about how hard it all was. By the time I got home, the bouncing pram had made Sienna forget whatever was bothering her and she was giggling and angelic again, a tiny arrow straight to my heart. It was exhausting, this up and down, this crumpling and expanding, this not knowing and should knowing and wondering how come everyone else seemed to know.

After that, I hardly met up with those women. The very women who had just gone through the same thing as me, who were as vulnerable and hopeful as me, who lived around the corner and were friendly and kind. I thought they were better at this mothering thing than me. They were relaxed and calm, and seemed to have endless hours to spend meeting up and walking by the sea, being paid while enjoying a year off work. Not me, with my own business. If I didn't show up I didn't get paid. I turned down invitation after invitation to meet for coffee, go jogging with our buggies, hang out at the library, 'come for tea'.

At the time I blamed it on my work – too busy, stuff to do, can't stop. But I think I was really hiding from the not knowing – who was I becoming? Why didn't I know what to do? Where did each day go? Why did my life feel out of control? I was scared that if I started to talk about it, I'd never stop and I'd completely unravel. So I said nothing, and kept working, and kept loving my baby and doing the chores and working some more, and feeling bad about how I didn't seem to get anything right anymore. And that's about all I did for the next year, until I got pregnant again, found myself on my bedroom floor, and decided that enough was enough.

RECONNECTING THE DISCONNECT

This particular experience was in the early days of motherhood, but I know from hundreds of conversations with people in my community that so many of us experience similar challenges in different aspects of our lives. Some disconnect from friends when they feel they aren't as successful as they 'should be'. Others have a sense of detachment from their old friendship circle when they realize they are interested in different things these days. Others put up walls of shame around money or broken relationships or any of the other things that are so often part of life. In the end, reconnecting with people I could really talk to was part of my escape, and it may well be part of yours too.

When I am feeling small and trapped and wooden and stuck, I find it really hard to reach out to others, even though that's often exactly what I need. Besides the practical reality of rarely leaving my house alone except to go for a walk or to a cafe to work, there's also the fear factor of getting to know new people. Because when people don't know me, they ask me questions about who I am and what I do. And when I'm feeling small and trapped and wooden and stuck, I'm not sure I know the answers.

But when I am feeling free, flying high, living in the moment and doing something I love, it's as if my kind of people are drawn towards me. I want to be out exploring and having interesting conversations, so I create opportunities to connect with like-minded people who want to do the same. In those moments those people energize and inspire me, giving me a glowing warmth, which is reflected back. In those moments I know exactly who I am and how to explain what I do in a way they will understand.

When I look back at that bedroom floor moment, I think I was lonely. But it was self-imposed because I had plenty of access to lovely people. The more I felt I wasn't doing things right, the more I retreated from everyone. I feared I'd be judged or rejected, if I admitted I didn't have it all together. I had always been the fiercely independent one who didn't need help. I mean, I was the one who helped others, not the one who asked for it, right? Who was I kidding?

Piece by piece, I started to reach out, first to my family then to a couple of friends and then further afield. Not everyone got it. Some people don't like to hear the hard parts. Perhaps they didn't want their version of me to be tarnished, so they didn't really listen and changed the subject as fast as they could. But some people (not always the ones I expected) recognized what I needed – true connection and genuine communication – and gave it to me. To them I will be forever grateful.

MEANINGFUL CONNECTIONS

The Freedom Key of Connection + Communication is about being and expressing your authentic self, and engaging with others in a meaningful way. It's about talking, and listening, and it's about the unsaid that is felt. It's about finding common ground, discovering what really matters and sharing that with others. It's about speaking your truth and standing in the power of that. It's about speaking from your brave heart to their brave heart. 'Here I am. There you are. I see you.' It's about radiating kindness in the way that you go through the world, both outward towards others, and inward towards yourself.

Connection + Communication is an important Freedom Key because if we don't communicate who we really are, and connect with others who appreciate us, we risk remaining forever trapped. We are creatures of words and empathy, kindness and friendship. Connecting makes us feel part of something greater than ourselves.

Genuine connection and authentic communication are not always easy. We have to open ourselves up to others, which can be intimidating. We have to listen, which can be hard. We have to pay attention, which isn't always the default. We have to find the words to say what we really mean, and take care when saying them out loud. Because what lives in the gaps, between the lines, unsaid, can be just as potent as what is spoken.

We are different people, seeing things from different perspectives, but our words have the power to bring us close, and help us help each other.

This Freedom Key can help when you feel you aren't being heard, or when you're skating on the surface without ever going deep. If you feel that you're drowning under the weight of everything, the right conversation can pull you out.

Within close relationships 'Connection + Communication' can help you find a way through the everyday chatter back to the strength of your original bond. It can also work miracles when you feel like you're hiding an aspect of yourself, trapped by secrecy, shame and guilt about something you aren't telling.

Even with those closest to us, sometimes we lose our way to each other in a sea of 'stuff' words – 'must do X, must buy Y, must remember Z' – a string of comments and motions that keep the wheels turning, but not the flame burning. We spend time alongside each other, without spending time with each other.

When we are trapped in the cage, we often use words as a form of defence. I find myself saying things that don't even sound like me. When I'm feeling hemmed in, I watch myself snap at my children or my husband and think, 'Where are these words coming from? Who is that talking in such a tone of voice?'

The way back is always through the eyes, the ears and the heart, really looking, listening and feeling. People can only help when you let them know you need it. It's so obvious and yet when the busyness takes over, it's so easy to forget or rush past. We are people, not robots. 'We are human beings not human doings,' as I saw graffitied on a wall somewhere by someone who clearly had too many things on their plate and no one to listen. I think Kurt Vonnegut said it first.

SECRETS HIDDEN BETWEEN THE LINES

Mr K and I share both family and working life, as we run our company together. Sometimes it's a blessing, sometimes a challenge. We usually manage well, juggling our family and running our business, one of us keeping the energy high if the other is flagging. But we haven't perfected it yet. I've noticed that when things go wrong, it's nearly always because we aren't paying attention to each other. And when things go right, it's nearly always because we are.

It's amazing what a difference a direct look in the eyes, a gentle smile, a small hand slipped into a bigger one, can make. For we were lovers and friends before we were parents and business owners. We need time for us, or else work and logistics take over. We often recalibrate over a coffee or check in while walking in the park with the girls asleep in their buggies. 'How are you? Any news? Tell me stuff.'

Often real conversation is a casualty of the speed at which we live, but sometimes it's simply because we don't really listen or connect, or we are just trying to have the conversation with the wrong people.

In Japanese the last half of a sentence is often left unsaid and the meaning is just implied. *Ikitain desu ga...* means 'I'd like to go but...' In English we'd feel compelled to give the reasons why we couldn't go even though we'd like to. In Japanese it's up to the listener to figure it out, to empathize and fill in the gaps. And to do that, they really have to listen, and feel beyond the words to the deeper meaning.

In every language there are secrets hidden between the lines, clues in the pauses and the tone, in the facial expressions and the body language. Real friendship grows from real conversation, which is as much about what isn't said, as what is. If you can navigate to your essence and speak from there, you can connect with the essence of others.

PAUSING ON THE THRESHOLD

Good communication is a work in progress, but I learned one of my most valuable lessons while taking tea.

The traditional tea ceremony in Japan is a thing of beauty, which compels you to yield to its delicate pace. Each ceremony has a host, who has their own sliding door, a *sadōguchi* to enter and exit the *chashitsu* (tea room) carrying the various utensils needed. The door is a simple wooden lattice frame with white paper affixed to both sides, which slides back with a gentle push, separating the tea room inside, and the corridor outside.

It always fascinated me how long it took for the kimono-clad host to get in and out of the room. They would kneel in the corridor, slide the door back, place their hands together in front of their knees with fingers to the floor and bow low, before rising to their feet and shuffling in, all in a reverential silence. This pause for bowing would give both the host and the guests a moment to acknowledge the outside and inside, the crossing of a boundary, the entry of each into the other's space.

Somehow this graciousness would allow the energy and atmosphere in the room to be held constant, regardless of the opening door and the entrance of another person. There was no sense of intrusion by the host or guests. No barging in, no loud introductions, no forced conversation. Simply a respectful pause at the threshold, and a silent invitation to share tea.

This 'threshold moment' had such an impact on me that I started translating it into my own life. Before I entered a room full of people I would take a moment to pause, consider who was inside and what the atmosphere was likely to be, and then enter. I felt a huge shift in the way I could read a room and how I was drawn to certain people without feeling like I was invading their space. I found the 'threshold moment' to be valuable in conversation too, to understand when to hold back and when to dive in.

It is especially useful now my house bustles with the energy of two small children. It is so easy to shout from the next room or burst in complaining about the leaking washing machine, without realizing you have just punctured the atmosphere of a carefully woven fairy tale, or disturbed father and daughter in the middle of an important conversation. I try not to open my mouth until I am in the same room, and if Mr K is playing with the girls I hover a moment in the doorway to see what they are doing before getting involved. Sometimes it's perfect for me to dive in too, but sometimes it's better to let them just be, and stand on the sidelines soaking in the beauty of the man I love deeply engaged with our children.

Often we switch from one part of our day straight into another, without a conscious transition. This means we take our work home, or our home stresses to work. We lunge from one meeting to the next, our bodies arriving before our minds. We turn up late for coffee with friends and swear about the traffic warden before we've even sat down, sabotaging the vibe created by those already gathered. Taking a moment to notice the shift from one place to another, to gauge the atmosphere and consciously arrive or leave makes all the difference.

Considering that 'threshold moment' takes practice, and even after years of doing it I still sometimes hang up the phone with an exasperated huff only to infect Mr K with my irritation, or burst into the room reeling off some story before realizing I have just shattered a delicate spell. But I try, and Mr K tries too, and it helps.

Besides helping us form bonds with others, outward listening allows us to soak up the beauty of the world and find our place in it. Inward listening helps us understand what's inside ourselves, and see who we are when everything is stripped away.

Being honest with ourselves is the only way to our truth. Communicating our truth is the path to authentic connection. And this brings huge rewards – deep friendship, love and support for our escape.

Often we hold back because we are scared of sharing too much and showing too much. But if we don't share and show and talk and listen, where's the connection, the caring, the humanity?

When you start to share who you really are, it may be uncomfortable for a while. Some people don't like surprises. Others won't relate to the 'new' version of you in the same way. But a short time of discomfort is better than a life in hiding.

Your people can only find you in the darkness when you shine your light brightly.

Activating the Connection + Communication Freedom Key

These days technology presents a paradox of connection. While it promises speed and efficiency and gives us access to more information, images and people than ever before, those very things can trap us when we start to compare our lives with other people's seemingly 'perfect' lives, spend endless hours checking in and give less to our lives offline.

Much of what makes this an 'advanced age' actually makes our lives more complex and difficult. Social media has forever changed the meaning of the word 'friend'. Electronic devices steal our attention, and we have fewer authentic connections with other human beings than ever. We are bombarded with advertising at every turn, which encourages us to take rather than give, consume rather than create, and makes us feel like we need to work harder and longer to pay for things we don't really need. These are the trends and patterns of modern society, and they are damaging us deeply. Can't we still the chatter and turn up the real conversation?

This isn't about rejecting technology, but rather choosing what to take and what to leave, when to tune in and when to switch off, when to look outward and when to look inward. To embrace the best of what is on offer, but use it to help our search for freedom, not hinder it. Sometimes disconnecting in one place allows us to better connect in another, with one another.

It's also not about trying too hard. So many of us shy away from talking to others, not knowing what to say and worrying that the conversation will feel forced. But sometimes doing something creative alongside someone else can be the catalyst for a lasting bond.

My friend Ali de John, founder of The Makerie, has witnessed this time and again. People join her creative workshops with the intention of learning how to make something, but as they work away alongside each other, that bond is quietly stitched. The parallel creative activity speaks volumes without words, connects without effort, and leaves a lasting glow of friendship.

If you are lacking genuine connection or real communication, try looking into someone's eyes properly as you talk to them. Stop what you're doing and really listen. What are they trying to tell you in the gaps and pauses, with their body language, with what they cannot say? Try having a real conversation about what freedom means to each of the people you really care about, and see where it takes you. When you speak, notice your tone of voice. Consciously change it, and see what happens. Be kind whenever you can.

There is a game Mr K and I often play on long car journeys. It's deceptively simple, but always yields surprising results. It's a great way in to what someone is really thinking. It's called 'Three Questions' and the only rules are:

- You ask each other three questions about absolutely anything, taking it in turns to ask and to answer.

- The person responding has to say whatever first comes to mind.

- You can't ask the same question back.

Often we ask silly questions like, 'What shoes would you pack if you were moving to Mars?' or 'Which rock star would you be if you could swap lives?' Sometimes we ask questions that bring us together with a shared memory, like 'What was the best curry you've ever eaten?'

But sometimes, just sometimes, the real things find their way in:

- If you could start over, what would you do differently?

- What is your favourite thing about us?

- What haven't you told me that you'd really like me to know?

- What makes you feel free?

The crucial skill is in the questions. First it's about bothering to ask, and then it's about what you actually ask.

Try starting a conversation with the intention to really connect, communicate and discover something, and see where it leads you.

Chapter 9

FREEDOM KEY 7: ENTERPRISE + INITIATIVE

Having taken the bold, brave step to create my book proposal, things happened fast. Within a few weeks I had an agent and a book deal with my dream publisher. The space I had created in my life was so expansive that this huge opportunity moved in to fill it. As I researched the book, tested my ideas, talked to hundreds of people and wrote, I discovered that the book itself wasn't the point. We set up our lives as a series of goals to achieve, and those goals are important for direction, but ultimately, ticking off one more thing is not as important as feeling free. And that's what the book was for me – a creative outlet that gave me an excuse to make more space, explore my other Freedom Keys and ultimately find my way back to feeling free.

The fact that a book brings with it new opportunities meant it opened up a new way to do what I love. And that's what the Freedom Key of Enterprise + Initiative is all about. It's about making your own rules, earning money how you want to and taking responsibility for your own future. It's about being smart, using your head and heart to decide what's right for you. For some people, it's about taking the leap to start their own business. For others it's about taking an enterprising approach to their career. For you, right now, it might just be about being open to a little more risk and a lot more possibility.

MAKING SHIFTS

I have used this Freedom Key whenever I've needed to make a shift in my career.

For example, several years ago, after working for UNICEF (see page 61), I left to become Head of Legacy Development for England's bid to host the 2018 FIFA World Cup. I was tasked with developing the plans for how England would use this sporting event for global good, if we were awarded the right to host. It was an extraordinary experience, which saw the English football industry collaborating in an unprecedented way. It felt like the tide might be turning within world sport, to really use its power for social good rather than just commercial gain.

FIFA (the world governing body of football) sent a technical team to scrutinize our bid. They described it as 'perfect', and the legacy plans as 'outstanding' and 'important for the future of world football'. We were riding high until FIFA's Executive Committee voted and England went out in the first round. We were dumbfounded, and desperately disappointed at the missed opportunity.

The bidding process had been overshadowed by dirty rumour, and many of the individuals involved have since been the subject of a large-scale investigation into corruption and misappropriation of funds. Maybe we'll never know the truth, but it made me sick to my stomach to think that a small group of self-interested people had stood in the way of a chance to do something amazing.

Of course I wanted us to win, but more than that I wanted sport to use its reach and popularity for good. I felt like all our work had been wasted, and completely lost faith that I could make the kind of contribution that I wanted, if I had to deal with people who abuse their power in that way. As a result, I decided to completely change direction in my professional life.

I turned my attention to working directly with individuals to help them achieve their full potential by doing something they love. I took the initiative to get out when things no longer felt right, and chose enterprise as a way not just to escape, but to flourish.

Since then my company, Do What You Love, has become a respected provider of online personal development courses that have been described numerous times as 'life-changing'. And I love it. But it hasn't all been a breeze.

When I started, I knew nothing about technology. I had never written an online course. I had never even written a blog post until a few months before I launched the company. But I clung on to what I believed and made the leap. The thing I wanted wasn't available, so I created it and made it a business to support my family financially, and several other families besides.

We create, produce and deliver online courses that help people all over the world find a new direction in life, monetize their passions and reorganize their life to focus on what makes them happy. We also teach people how to create their own online courses and run online businesses, because this opens up the whole world to them. I have seen how, with the right tools and guidance, and with today's technology, anyone can carve out the life they want. It takes time and commitment, but it is more possible than ever. Many of our online course graduates have gone on to start their own businesses or make a very comfortable living teaching online. Through our partnerships www.makeartthatsells.com and www.makeitindesign.com we have also helped thousands of artists and designers flourish in professional creative careers.

Of course we have met a host of naysayers along the way – they are easy to spot with their screwed-up foreheads, shaking heads and air of superiority. They are the same ones who advise young people to get a 'safe job' with a big salary, and scare them away from the idea of pursuing their passion in case it doesn't pay. I get the economics, but what about the human experience? And if you love something you'll probably be better at it, or at least more committed to it, so in the long run you'll have a greater chance of doing well in it anyway.

And if you love it, you can enjoy all the steps along the way, rather than slave away at something you dislike in the hope that one day you'll have enough money to retire and finally start to enjoy your life.

Your life is happening right here, right now, and we need more careers (and life) advice which recognizes that.

We carry on regardless of the naysayers, because we know the secret: Living more, worrying less and doing what you love is a path to happiness. It puts you in the driving seat and makes you responsible for your own success, as defined by you. It allows you to use all of your skills and experience, work with and for people who light you up, and find meaning and purpose in your days.

Life is too short to spend it doing something you don't love, with unfulfilled potential and faraway dreams. You don't have to be the boss, but you can take a strategic approach to your own life and use your initiative to start choosing what you really want.

Give yourself permission to do what you love, and in doing so you'll give others permission to do the same.

BEING OPEN TO POSSIBILITY

Never before have we had greater opportunities to do what we love or more options for ways to go about it. These days, making money from our passions is a business plan, not a pipe dream.

What if I told you working for yourself in the right business, or taking the initiative to leap to a new career with the right organization, could buy you more time and less stress? What if I assured you it could give you more flexibility, less bureaucracy, more income, more purpose and more reward?

These are the gifts of Enterprise + Initiative: the rewards for stepping into your power, making choices that serve you and bringing your work to the world.

When you know you can no longer go on working and earning the same way or want more flexibility and influence over your own earning capacity and direction, this Freedom Key can help you take the first step.

Activating the Enterprise + Initiative Freedom Key

Think about whether any of the concepts below appeal to you, and if so, imagine what might be different about your life if this was your reality:

1. Following your dreams and seeing them come true.

2. Doing something you love.

3. Turning your ideas into something that makes you proud.

4. Being responsible for your own professional and financial destiny, not relying on anyone else for 'security'.

5. Earning money based on what you have created, not how many hours you have put in, or whether you made an appearance at the office.

6. Not answering to anyone else.

7. Not having to work with anyone you don't like.

8. Working from wherever you choose.

9. Sharing your knowledge, experience and gifts through teaching, either online or offline.

10. Earning money while you sleep.

11. Expanding your income streams so you earn money from several places.

12. Being master of your own time, fitting work around life, not the other way around.

The Freedom Key of Enterprise + Initiative unlocks all these possibilities. When you're trapped in the cage, this is not about rushing out to start your own business or quitting your job without thinking it through. It's about planting the seed of possibility, exploring ideas, taking initiative, doing some research and contemplating what applying an enterprising spirit could do for you. Considering the possibilities alerts your subconscious to the fact that you are open to alternative paths.

‿

Chapter 10

FREEDOM KEY 8: GRATITUDE † CONSCIOUS LIVING

The escape process made me realize that I already had a lot to be grateful for. In paying more attention to that, I found myself living more consciously, taking note of the details, and in doing so, discovering even more blessings.

When you get into a gratitude habit, it can shift your mindset and boost your happiness. Even then, it's easy to let life take over once more and miss the everyday miracles until a gritty experience reminds you, yet again, of what you have to be grateful for.

Take my friend Ella (name changed for privacy). She's been trying for a baby for several years and finally got pregnant a short while back. There was such happiness surrounding the news. But this morning she went for a 12-week scan and they couldn't find a heartbeat. On hearing the pain in her voice, the air is sucked out of the room and my heart feels like a machine gun hammering against my ribs. People say they feel empty when they have lost something, but I am so sad for her I feel filled up with it. She wanted that baby so much.

On the phone just now we talked about how she did everything she could to provide a healthy nurturing place for the baby to develop, how this is a step in the right direction for someone who didn't know if she could get pregnant at all, how maybe there is another soul waiting to be born to her in the future. I am sure none of it helps. It doesn't take away the raw pain of knowing that her little baby's heart stopped beating. That at some point its heart beat for the last time, perhaps when she was washing up, or sleeping, or thinking how much she was going to love her child. I couldn't do anything to soften her pain. All I could do was be in it with her.

As happens when you hear any sad news, you can't help reflecting on your own situation, and the faces of my two girls are blurry through my tears. Sienna is at nursery and Maia is with her grandma today, so I can concentrate on work, only I can't concentrate on anything except this news, how heartbroken I am for my friend, and how grateful I am for my children.

In this moment I don't care about the tantrums or the teething or the sleepless nights. I just want to wrap them in my love, and more than anything I want that for my friend.

I want her to be able to make another baby, to play host to another soul, to be the mother she has already started to become. I'm wishing, hoping, sending her love on this dark day, my ear hot from the telephone conversation and my heart heavy as bricks.

I head home full of second-hand sadness, casting a long shadow in the winter sun. But I don't dawdle, I hurry. I need to gather up my own girls and hold them to me. I have never felt more grateful for them than in this moment.

But within a few days, life takes over and I forget. In the everyday chaos my recognition of their preciousness gets left in the pocket of my coat like a used theatre ticket, and I get frustrated with unimportant things once again.

At the end of a particularly long day I am soaking in a hot bath when I hear the door swing open and tiny feet come running in.

'Oh come on, can't I get even five minutes of peace?'

Sienna reaches up and over the tub and starts washing my back with her little sponge. She puts her hand in the water.

'Hot.' Then she puts her hand in the bubbles. 'Not hot.'

I have never noticed that.

'Mummy need toys.' It's not a question. She passes me her favourite yellow watering can. She has foam on her nose and a look of deep concentration on her face. The ends of her fine blonde hair are curling in the heat.

'Water on Sienna's toes,' she says, squeezing her sponge and watching the drips fall. 'Feet grow big like Daddy.'

My heart swells with the beauty of her gift and the sincerity with which it is given. This is what matters.

Living consciously, in the moment, allows me to notice her preciousness once again, and be grateful for it. The gift in the context of motherhood was staring right at me, and had been there all along.

BEING AWARE OF WHAT YOU HAVE

The Freedom Key of Gratitude + Conscious Living is about being aware of what you already have, being open to giving and receiving, and being thankful for it all. It's about understanding the impact of our actions and finding ways to appreciate that we get to be here, in this lifetime, living this life.

Why do we stop living consciously in the first place? How did I get to that bedroom floor moment, where I was so caught up in the stuff I had to do, that I forgot about the experience of living itself? It is our choice to allow the pace to keep increasing, to allow others to set our markers of success, to succumb to the pressure. But ultimately we can also choose not to be accountable to those things, and instead be accountable to our own version of a good life.

When something bad happens we often tuck it away in a shoebox at the back of a cupboard and try to forget about it. But all that does is numb us. And if we numb anything, we numb it all. In numbing the sadness we numb the delight. If we open up to the pain and the vulnerability, we open up to the grace and the beauty. When we notice all we already have, in all areas of our lives, we feel grateful, and that gratitude floods our hearts with warmth and love. It plugs us into the very experience of our own lives, rather than letting those lives just rush past.

Living consciously means:

- ❀ Choosing how we spend every precious day.
- ❀ Living according to our values.
- ❀ Mindfully choosing what we eat, how we travel, who we spend our time with, where we spend our energy, how we

relax, how we consume, how we talk, how we love, how we show compassion, how we try to be kind.

✤ Being aware of how we feel, acknowledging it, and then letting ourselves feel it.

✤ Being prepared to receive.

Be grateful for even the tiniest of miracles because they add up to this thing called life.

Emerging from the wave

Lotus Zalzala used to be a real-life playboy. He made a fortune in his thirties selling electronic components. He had offices all over the world and a jet-set lifestyle to match. When the weekend came, he would often take off to Vegas and party his way through to Monday. He worked 80 hours a week, had status, good looks, glamorous friends and more money than he could ever need. The world hailed him a success story. But something wasn't right. He couldn't work out why, with everything he had, he felt so empty.

One day in 2005 he developed a really bad rash on his back. It turned out to be shingles. His body was trying to tell him his way of life was not sustainable. He was prescribed rest, so he took himself to the Bahamas, where an old friend ran a B&B and lived slowly. At first the pace was unsettling, but when Lotus eventually surrendered to it, he started to feel better. He carried on working, but started shunning parties in favour of travel.

On one trip to Mexico he was out surfing when a wave crashed over him. As he tumbled underwater, he felt a shooting pain in his arm which fired a message direct to his brain: he wasn't indestructible. He had broken his elbow and it was a painful reminder that his actions had an impact on his body. He had been so plugged into the grid, into the high-rolling life and making money that he had completely disconnected from his inner self and the body that housed it. He emerged from that wave fully awake, knowing what he needed to do to save his life. Healing took many months and the loving support of a close friend who encouraged him to explore who he really was deep down.

He sold his company and moved to Costa Rica, where he fell in love with a different kind of bounty. He cleaned out everything. He sobered up, became a raw vegan, trained as a yoga teacher and even turned to celibacy, giving up everything he had thought was important, to discover what really was.

Little more than five years on and he is a different person. Or, more accurately, he is the same person. The different person he became for a while has gone for good. His parents don't quite get it yet and his old friends don't really call anymore, but that is a small sacrifice for someone who has navigated towards his essence and found freedom by living consciously.

LIVING CONSCIOUSLY

I started to think about what my day would look like if I lived every moment consciously and gratefully with all my senses, focusing on the beauty and preciousness of each moment, not tying everything to some potential future reward, or allowing fear to make choices for me.

When I tried it, the plan I dreamed up for my day went something like this:

Today I will do only things that celebrate the most important things and people in my life.

I will share crispy toast with Sienna and we'll take it in turns to dip the soldiers into sticky jam, and who cares about the crumbs.

I will take her for a walk by the river and she will look to the sky and see that the moon is missing. She will point to the trees and say Mr Moon is in there, having a picnic, and tell me she wants to bring him strawberry tea. I will watch the hazy smudges of dark and light on the surface of the river, as those same trees are reflected, and catch a flash of silver as a pike darts below.

I will spin Maia round and round and tickle her soft tummy until her giggles ring out across the land. I will drink in her sweetness and nuzzle her wispy golden hair.

I will take my husband's hand as we walk and kiss him a hundred times. I will write a letter, bake a cake, walk barefoot on the grass, call my parents, turn my face to the sun.

I will breathe deeply, laugh loudly, write freely, move my body, nurture my family and, at the end of the day I will lie on the ground and look up at the stars, gaze in wonder, imagine myself looking down from up there and seeing me down here looking up, and let my mind expand to the infinite vastness of the sky.

Today I will be grateful for a very good day.

Day-to-day happiness is a registration of all the delicious moments that happen when we are feeling free. It's about a willingness to be delighted and joyful at any given moment, to find the gift in the challenge, the diamond in the sand.

The Freedom Key of Gratitude + Conscious Living is helpful anytime and all the time. When we are grateful and live consciously, we are thankful for the choices we have made and confident in those choices. This in turn makes us appreciate our own power.

It can be particularly helpful when you are consumed with worry, because paying more attention to the details of your life as it is right now can help you find the goodness in it, as well as distracting you from the circuitous dialogue in your head. And using this Freedom Key means when you escape the cage, you will launch consciously from a positive place of gratitude.

Activating the Gratitude + Conscious Living Freedom Key

Noticing starts with the senses. We use our senses for many things - for orienting ourselves in the world around us, for safety, for pleasure. They can prompt action, affect our moods, influence our impressions of others, spark fear, anticipation or memories.

Do you take your senses for granted, or use them consciously? How often do you literally stop and smell the flowers?

- Step outside for a moment and think about what the weather is like today. What does it look like? What colour is it? What does it sound like? What does it smell like? How does it make you feel? What memories does it stir up? What does it make you want to do?

- Imagine yourself as a raindrop or as the wind or as the sun beaming down. How does the earth look different from that perspective?

- Watch the clouds move across the sky. Where are they going? What can they see?

Something as simple as thinking about the weather can invoke a sense of wonder and possibility, make you notice new things, and prompt new thoughts and ideas.

Make a list of five things you're grateful for today. If you regularly practise gratitude, then today extend that to telling someone what you're grateful for in them.

As you go about your day, as far as possible, be conscious of the decisions you make, the interactions you have, the things you ask for, give and receive, what you eat, when and how you move, the thoughts you entertain. Where possible choose kindness, to yourself, and to others. See what difference it makes.

Chapter 11

FIT TO FLY: EMERGING INTO THE WORLD + LEARNING HOW TO FLY

After all that exploration, what are your master keys? Which Freedom Keys were you drawn to? Which were obvious first choices for you? Which offered an unexpected way out? How did it feel to lead your mind away from thinking about the cage bars, to a point where the focus of your thoughts started to change?

If you have tried one or two and still feel stuck, try another and another, until you find the Freedom Key that unlocks the door of your cage right now. Don't presume you know the answer. Different Freedom Keys will serve you best at different times.

If the Freedom Key you were first drawn to isn't working for you, it might be due to trying to retrofit your current life into a past version of it. Instead try finding a way that works in this moment, knowing that next week, next month, next year, you might need to activate a particular Freedom Key in a completely different way, or choose a different Freedom Key altogether.

When I'm stuck and I journal, I come back to the same themes over and over. I need space, quiet, time to write, time in nature, proper time with my family, good food, exercise, inspiring conversation, the promise of adventure, a moment to be grateful. You may need these things too, or you may need something entirely different. Whatever you need you will find the essence of it every time you return to the Freedom Keys.

It's easy to feel guilty for doing things that on the surface might seem selfish and have little or no immediate tangible result. But if you can connect the action to a Freedom Key, it can help you see the bigger picture. You realize it's not selfish, but self-care.

Take small steps and be patient. It's important to escape the cage before you try to fly. Otherwise you'll get inspired, take off, but then smash up against the cage bars and get frustrated all over again.

Get out first. Take off later.

One step at a time. Find the key. Open the door.

Move away from the darkness and the stuckness, towards the lightness, and the light.

EMERGING

When a bird or an animal in captivity is released into the wild, it doesn't burst out of its cage and race headlong into its new world. It emerges timidly, often looking back several times at the cage that has kept it 'safe', before it tentatively moves away.

On occasion birds and animals have been seen to celebrate joyously upon release from captivity, but in most cases they hover near their cage, clearly stunned by the reality of their new situation. The truth is, even though the door is open, the cage is still there. They know they have to make the choice to leave, but they are terrified of the unknown. They have no idea what to do or where to go.

And so it is with us. We're rarely trapped one moment and free the next. We're rarely ready to soar as soon as the door opens. And the cage doesn't usually disappear as soon as we leave it. The reality is more complex. We hover at the door, tempted forwards by potential but held back by fear.

Metamorphosis

When I returned home from the art retreat I mentioned in Chapter 6, Mr K said I was like a firefly, flitting around excitedly, emitting bursts of light. The high lasted a good 48 hours until it eventually faded and I was left languishing in the dark.

All I wanted to do was make art, but every time I tried, it didn't look like the art I wanted to make. I needed somehow to describe what had just happened, but when I stared at the art supplies that had seemed so full of potential in California, and the book I made while there, they didn't add up to the colossal experience I had just had.

In amongst those giant redwoods, on that ancient tribal land, something had happened to me from the inside out. If you had watched from above you would have just seen a girl having fun, cutting and sticking and painting and laughing. But if you had come close and looked into my eyes you would have seen a pool of wonder, my heart fluttering a little faster, my mind whirring with new possibility. I could feel a wholly unanticipated expansion, an opening, a revealing of a brave new world.

But back home I felt all at sea. I knew I could never go back to the way things were, separated from my creativity, but I also had no idea what to do next. I had opened the cage door but was teetering on the ledge, with no idea of where or how to fly.

At that art retreat, I experienced a number of a-ha moments and went home forever shifted. But the actual change from my old life to my new cracked-open life was not an overnight transformation. When I arrived back from the USA, I didn't disembark from the plane as someone who believed they could legitimately have a creative career as soon as they'd unpacked. Although I definitely dared to dream it might be possible one day, I was far from confident and a long way from making it happen.

In the end it took several months of exploring, journaling, taking classes, trying new things, and searching for my version of creativity, to start making sense of the metamorphosis.

The next couple of years were a time of emergence, with some major moves forward, some debilitating backward steps, many happy moments, some lost moments, times of joy, times of shattered confidence and a persistent wondering what in hell I thought I was doing.

You see, the caterpillar doesn't know what's happening when he's in the cocoon. He doesn't know that the ache in his shoulders is the cartilage of his wings hardening. He doesn't know that the tightening around his body is the swelling of his wing feathers, as they develop the markings that will identify him in the next phase of his life. He doesn't understand the strange feeling in his scalp as his antennae push up and out. He is asleep through the entire transformation process, dreaming of leaves and raindrops and sunshine.

The day he emerges from his cocoon he senses an unfolding. He looks different. He feels different. He is capable of new things. Instead of just leaves, he is now drawn to a new kind of beauty in flowers, which he starts to see everywhere. He flutters around testing out his new wings, which had been hidden inside all along. Only then does he know what to do in his new life.

For me the shift had been so huge, I knew that one day I would want to earn my living in a more creative way, but for the time being I stayed in my job to let myself explore without the pressure of trying to make it pay. It felt safer that way. I'm not normally one to go for the safe option, but this was completely uncharted territory and I had no idea what lay ahead.

Whether or not you fly depends on what you do at the threshold of your cage. Will you teeter at the edge and allow your fear to keep you trapped, or will you step out into the unknown, buoyed by the promise of what lies beyond? Remember our definition:

> *Freedom is the willingness and ability to choose your own path and experience your life as your true self.*

On returning home from that art retreat I felt a force greater than myself sweeping me towards this new way of being. Towards the freedom of a more creative, inspired life, sharing myself with the world in small and big ways, because I had opened myself up to it. But I was terrified.

TAKING THE LEAP

When you're at the entrance to the cage, you get a sensation that could be either terror or excitement – two feelings that are physically very similar, but differentiated by the lens through which you view them. The fear response makes you shrink back, the excited response makes you advance forward.

When I discussed this with my wise friend, mindfulness expert Rohan Gunatillake, he reminded me that when we just escape life temporarily, by taking a holiday or obliterating reality with substances for example, we aren't actually free. All we are doing is turning away from the cage bars so we cannot see them, but we are still trapped.

At a time like this, when you're trying to emerge from the cage, Rohan suggests you ask yourself, 'What am I open to here?' That allows you to turn yourself towards the experience rather than back away from it, which subsequently allows an opening, and a change.

DARE TO STEP OUT OF THE CAGE

In the two years following that initial art retreat I went back to the USA twice for two other workshops, started a blog, quit the industry I knew, started Do What You Love, ran my own retreat, created my first online course, got published in a magazine and one day realized that everything I had scribbled in my journal under those redwoods was actually happening. I was manifesting my own dreams, but only because I had dared to step out of the cage. For a logic-loving scientific-minded sceptic like me, this was a revelation, and if I can do it, so can you.

When the caterpillar metamorphoses, he isn't wasting time deciding whether to become a Red Admiral or a Silver-Studded Blue. His destiny – as a creature capable of flight – is already decided for him. That capacity is already in him, waiting to emerge. His job is simply to find a way to become it.

We have to go through this phase of everything not quite fitting, not quite making sense, in order to emerge as the extraordinary artwork that we are destined to become.

Mess births beauty.
Chaos is progress.

Knowing this is a great relief, because when it feels like nothing is working, when you've forgotten how you got here and what you're trying to do, that's when you know it's actually working perfectly.

You've come this far. Don't back away now. It's time to step off the ledge and into your life, from small and trapped to vast and free. That cage door is a gateway to freedom, framing all the potential and possibility that lies ahead.

Entry 8: Letting it happen

Once you have used your Freedom Keys to help you open the cage door, it's likely that you will feel all at sea for a while. Pay attention to this, because it's an important indicator of growth and emergence. Get quiet and journal your responses to the following questions:

1. *How do you feel at the threshold of your cage? What are you excited about? What are you unsure of?*

2. *Do you feel any forces pushing or pulling you out into the big wide world?*

3. *Do you feel any forces pushing or pulling you back into the cage?*

4. *If a friend was where you are right now, what would you say to encourage them?*

5. *How do you feel knowing that this is just part of the process, and it's meant to be happening?*

6. *What are you open to here?*

LETTING GO AND LOSING CONTROL

One of the scariest things about life outside the bars is the great unknown. If we are used to running the show inside the cage, how can we cope outside it, when we don't even know what's coming next?

It reminds me of a sweet folktale about the sun and the wind, which my mum told me when I was a little girl and having a tantrum about wearing my navy-blue duffle coat.

The sun and the wind were bored. They were up in the sky looking down, with nothing much to do, so the wind said to the sun, 'Let's play a game. You see that little girl down there in the blue coat? I bet you I can make her take that coat off before you can.'

'OK,' said the sun. 'But I'll win.'

'No chance,' said the wind. 'I am so much stronger than you. I can bend tree trunks, rattle windows and power sails. I will make her take it off.'

So the wind blew, and blew. But the little girl just pulled her coat round her and did up the buttons. She bent her head and pushed back against the wind.

'What's happening? I don't understand.' said the wind, dejected.

'My turn now,' said the sun. And he beamed and beamed, shining brighter and warming the earth. The little girl looked up and smiled, then undid the toggles, wriggled out of her coat and skipped on down the road.

'How did you do that?' asked the wind.

'I didn't try to force her to take her coat off,' the sun said wisely. 'I made her want to do it.'

❧

And that is the difference between power and control. Freedom is about harnessing your power while letting go of the need to always be in control.

Think about the word 'control' for a minute. Doesn't it feel tight, grasping, manipulative and ugly? It's exhausting to try to control everything and ultimately it isn't sustainable. You just create stress trying to micromanage other people, second-guessing reactions and juggling too many things. Think of the wind in the story, with his red puffy cheeks and deep frown.

Now think about 'letting go'. Doesn't that feel better? More relaxing, gentle, inspiring? It's about trusting, being gentle, allowing. Think of the sun with his wide smile and warm sunbeams.

We can't control the movement of the planets, the changing seasons or the growing of our own fingernails. We can't control what family we are born into, our upbringing or whether we win the lottery. So why do we think we can control how other people think, what they do or what happens tomorrow? The fact is, while we can make choices that influence outcomes, we cannot control those outcomes. Once you know it's not possible you stop trying, and with that comes sweet relief.

Focus on what you can control – your cage bars, your responses and reactions, your mindset, your attitude, your choices, your escape plan – instead of what you often cannot control – your context, the people in it and pretty much everything else.

If you're a self-confessed 'control freak', don't worry, your obsessive tendencies have prepared you well. You have a lot of energy, you are proactive and smart, and you have superb organizational skills. All those things can serve you if you direct them towards feeling free. Just think how much more time you'll have, when you aren't trying to run everything, do everything, think of everything.

Letting go of the need to always be in control doesn't mean not having a plan. Planning is actually an essential skill of the

Freedom Seeker, as you will see later. Rather, letting go means being open to what might happen, being ready for when it does and enjoying the process along the way.

Surrendering control doesn't mean becoming powerless. The exact opposite, in fact. It's how we become powerful.

So often we give away our power to others, but we need to claim it and use it. We can serve without being subservient. We must stand up, not shrink back. We have too much to give to be hidden. And we can use that power to choose the attitude we have towards every part of our lives.

Exercising your personal power allows you to make the choices that will set you free. And losing the need for control opens you up to possibility, serendipity and miracles. So release your need for control, and relax into the ease and contentment of allowing life to unfold.

WHEN THINGS DON'T GO TO PLAN

But what happens if you make a bold move and it doesn't work out? What if you quit your job, leave a toxic relationship or start a new business, and find yourself afraid, doubting, back to square one? How confusing. If you follow your instincts and things don't work out, what then? You wonder where you went wrong, lose all confidence and shrink back.

But there is a very simple reason why this happens. It's because we assume that escaping the cage is the end of the story, when actually it's the beginning.

We forget that we have to learn how to fly again.

THE MECHANICS OF FLIGHT

In order to fly, a bird needs to balance two pairs of opposing forces – weight (down) with lift (up), and drag (backward) with thrust (forward).

We can relate this to life and our own efforts to 'fly'.

The vertical forces of weight and lift are concerned with what lies within:

❋ The **weight** is represented by the words of your **inner critic**, pulling you down. It is in perfectionism and worry, self-doubt and fear.

❋ This can be counteracted with **lift**, the guidance from your **inner sage**, the kind but quiet voice inside which gently encourages and motivates you, the knowing that lifts you up. It is self-confidence, self-trust and self-belief.

The horizontal forces of **drag** and **thrust** are in the relationships and interactions you have with other people:

❋ **Drag** is represented by the **negative impact of other people** on your confidence, convictions and actions. It is in their jealousy, naysaying and bullying. It is wing-clipping, dream-crushing, trust-breaking and disapproval.

❋ **Thrust** is represented by the **positive impact of other people** on your confidence, convictions and actions. It is in their support, reassurance, comfort and cheerleading. It is accountability, trust and love.

When you are weighed down more than you are lifted up, you cannot take off – and when you let the drag outweigh the thrust, you cannot move forward. We will look at each of these forces in turn, because with awareness comes the power to choose which force gets your attention.

The mechanics of flight is all about how we can choose to sabotage our own potential, or allow others to do that, or choose to fly high, and surround ourselves with people who will help us fly higher.

It's all a choice. What will you choose?

Vertical forces: Weight + Lift

You have a huge influence on your own flight potential. You can allow your inner critic to rule, and get weighed down by your insecurities and the baggage you carry around.

Or you can allow your inner sage to guide you, and be buoyed by the kind but quiet voice inside which gently lifts you and shows you the way.

Entry 9: Weight + Lift

Open your journal and draw a simple sketch in the middle of a new page, depicting a bird flying left to right. If you don't like drawing, find a picture of a bird in flight and stick it in there, or download a bird template from www.bethkempton.com/flyfree.

Draw four arrows emanating from your bird, one pointing up, one down, one pointing forward, one backward.

Below the downward arrow list everything in your head that is still weighing you down, even though you have made the initial step of escaping the cage. This is the voice of your inner critic.

Above the upward arrow list everything about you that you have confidence in and which lifts you up. This is the voice of your inner sage. If you can't think of much to say, don't worry, the next exercise will help you with that.

Leave the other arrows blank for now. We will come back to them in Entry 16 (see page 161).

NOBODY'S PERFECT

When I was 17 my parents gave me birthday money for driving lessons. I spent it all on clothes. I went to university in a small town where I didn't need a car, and then I lived in Tokyo, where everyone gets around by underground. So I didn't start learning to drive until my mid-twenties, but it was a disaster from the beginning.

For some reason I had a major complex about the fact I couldn't drive. I learned in secret and failed my first test in secret. By the time I failed my second test, driving had become a taboo subject. I would get snappy whenever anyone mentioned driving lessons and felt completely useless anytime I saw a teenager racing down the road.

Soon after I had failed for the second time, I accidentally blurted it out to my younger brother Matt. He cheered. Huh?

'I failed, as in, I didn't pass.' I said, thrown by his congratulatory response.

'I know,' he replied. 'You never fail anything. Now I know you're human.'

What was he talking about? I failed things all the time. Then I realized I tended to share what I had done recently, but rarely what I was doing at the time, or thinking about doing in the future. I am generally a positive person, so I tended to share good news, rather than complain about things. But it was also because I'm a (recovering) perfectionist, so back then I would only share the things that had gone well, not the messy works-in-progress.

Unbeknown to me, the result was that I looked like I always had everything together, always getting what I aimed for and never failing. The truth, of course, was very different, but no one knew. The result? If I went for something and it didn't work out, I'd have to handle the stress and stew in my disappointment alone.

As soon as I told Matt about my failed driving test and how I had almost turned right into the oncoming traffic on a dual carriageway, I started laughing. By the time I explained the look of sheer horror on the examiner's face and the moment I knew my test was doomed when he grabbed the steering wheel, I had tears streaming down my face. I was laughing at myself and realized that it really didn't matter that I had failed again. Of course it was an inconvenience, but it didn't make me a worse person. It just made me someone who needed to concentrate more next time around.

Ever since then I've tried to be more open about the things I am aiming for, as I go for them, instead of only sharing if things work out. It's harder, and it makes me feel vulnerable, but my experience is richer for doing so. It's real life in all its messy beauty, not an airbrushed version of it. Letting go of perfectionism releases weight, and allows others to support your flight.

If freedom is about being willing and able to choose your own path, and experience it as your true self, then being willing and able to share that journey with others must be a crucial part of it. Nobody is perfect, and it's in witnessing each other's failures and disappointments and vulnerability and truth that we really connect with each other. And it's only when we do so that we can help each other to fly free.

BANISHING SELF—DOUBT

When I began my business, online courses were still relatively new and I knew very little about technology. But with a lot of trial and error, and the help of some patient friends, I created the Do What You Love e-course. It was something of a pioneering concept, which meant there weren't many others to learn from, so I had to work it out as I went along.

Back then the e-course included written posts, my photography, exercises and weekly audio recordings. Deep down I knew I should have video content too, but I was too terrified to contemplate producing my own short films.

So I ran the course without video several times, with astonishing results. People were sending me emails, letters and gifts in the post, saying that the course had been life-changing for them. Some had made major changes – quit their jobs, started their own businesses, moved continents, got married, got divorced even – while others had made smaller but important changes which helped them find more joy in their daily lives.

When I first started getting this feedback, I thought they were just being polite. But soon I realized it was real. They were taking my teaching and running with it, being bold and brave, pushing their own boundaries and choosing how to live. I was hugely inspired, and totally intimidated. My students were pushing themselves, but why wasn't I?

Every time I ran the course I had a niggling feeling that it was really missing something by not having video content, and other video-led e-courses were starting to pop up. I also felt that I had grown significantly since I first wrote it. The time had come for an overhaul. So I decided to add video. The only thing was I was pregnant with my first child, and I didn't want to date the videos with my pregnant belly in maternity clothes, so I booked a film crew for a few months after my due date. And then I had my baby and forgot all about it.

Sienna arrived two weeks late, on Christmas Day. As a result, I had consumed my body weight in Christmas cake, and was around 20kg heavier than usual. I was also exhausted, pasty and hadn't been to the hairdresser for months. And then I remembered the filming, just a few weeks away.

I couldn't do it. I'd have to wait until I was thinner and more confident. I told Mr K we'd have to cancel the film crew, the makeup artist, the photographer and the boat we'd chartered to film on. He wasn't keen. It would cost a lot in fees, and would delay the relaunch of the course, with a knock-on effect for the company's finances.

'But I'm not ready,' I moaned. 'Look at the state of me. I'm fat. My head is mush. And I'm so busy juggling everything that I'm actually a terrible example of doing what you love right now.'

As always, Mr K let me finish and then smiled. 'First, you've just had a baby, and you're doing brilliantly.'

'Secondly, do you really think your students are watching the video to see how thin you are? Or how perfect your life is? They want to see you because they want to be seen. They want to know you care enough to get on camera and talk to them. They want you to tell your stories, so they can better relate to theirs. They come to the course because you have lived your stories, because you have been through what they are going through, and because you're guiding them from a place of vulnerability and experience, not because you have everything together.

'It's enough just to get on camera and talk to them. Be yourself. Share what you know. Throw your scripts out and just say what you want to say. It's enough to be just as you are right now.'

Can you see why I married him? He's pretty wise.

It was a massive a-ha moment. The videos weren't about me at all. The self-doubt wasn't serving anyone, least of all my students, who I really wanted to support. Although I'm always going to take the opportunity for professional makeup any time I'm on camera, the rest of it really doesn't matter that much. I didn't need to wait until my brain was clear enough to remember every sentence of a script. I didn't need to wait until the eye bags were gone or I was three dress sizes smaller. (Thank goodness. The students would have been waiting a long time.)

I have enough, know enough and am enough as I am. My job is simply to show up and serve.

I AM ENOUGH

Every time I start to doubt myself I sit myself down and say, 'What's your job here? What really matters? Who are you serving with your self-doubt? How could you serve people better without it?'

Self-doubt is heavy: 'I'm not smart enough. I'm not prepared enough. I'm not beautiful enough. I'm not lovable enough. I'm not qualified enough. I'm not good enough.' But I want to ask you this: 'Not good enough for what? Not good enough for who?' If you know that you're doing your best, then you are doing enough already.

This doesn't mean you don't need to try. I'm a big advocate of putting time and effort into bringing my ideas to life, because that's part of doing my best. But sometimes, actually most of the time, I feel there is more I could have done. I could have read that briefing one more time, spent another hour crafting that blog post, got to the gym more this week and so on. But you can only do what you can do.

If you're doing your best, that's enough. If you know you could do better, but not right now, that's enough right now. If you bring love to the table every time, that's plenty.

We are enough. Just as we are.

Entry 10: Say hello

If we let our inner critic run wild, we get caught up in our thoughts and build up layer upon layer of worry and judgement. 'I'm worried about failing. I'm worried about the fact that I'm worried. I'm such a loser for worrying so much.' And on and on.

But it is possible to do the opposite. Creator of award-winning mindfulness app 'buddhify', Rohan Gunatillake knows that practising mindfulness and meditation can quieten the mind, and help you become aware of your thoughts, separating yourself from them. He believes that once you become a neutral observer, you start to relate to your thoughts in a different way, so when you see them rising up you can actively work to diffuse them.

Rohan taught me this simple but hugely effective exercise, and has kindly allowed me to share it with you.

1. *When you doubt yourself or feel worried, take a moment to listen to your thoughts.*

2. *As each one comes up, name it. You might want to use its actual name, like 'Worry', 'Self-bashing', 'Guilt', etc. Or you might want to be playful and give it a unique name, like 'Story of Woe', 'Mr Demotivator' or whatever you like.*

3. *Then greet it. Say out loud, 'Hello, Money Worry. I see you there.'*

In order to name it, you have to observe it, so you have to separate from the thought and give yourself some space. By greeting it, you soften its impact.

Every time you notice yourself worrying, or doubting yourself, try this and make a note in your journal about what difference it makes.

SEEING THE FULL PICTURE

Many of us don't see the gold in our experiences. We don't realize that our vulnerability is the key to connecting with others. We don't acknowledge that our 'failures' are actually hugely valuable lessons. This has never been so clearly demonstrated to me as when I met a real-life clown.

∼ The glimmer of gold ∼

Allan Girod was working as a history teacher in a small town in Western Australia when he was dragged into the local amateur dramatics society. A self-confessed 'super-introvert', Allan was terrified, but the moment he stepped onto the stage he came alive. Performing allowed him to pretend that he wasn't shy and that he didn't care what others thought of him. In character, Allan was larger than life and he loved it.

After a particularly challenging year of teaching, Allan decided to quit and try acting full time. Despite having no formal training, he went straight into a job in a production of Road Train. *The show had rave reviews and gave Allan a real taste of acting, but after a while he lost confidence in himself and quit to work as a tour guide. He began with basic tours, but as his experience and reputation grew, he found himself leading adventures into the Australian Outback. One day a traveller fell ill and, although Allan coped, he realized that he felt wholly unqualified for what he was doing.*

This is a recurring theme for Allan: he dives in without thinking, which allows him to be bold and brave, but after a while his rational mind catches up and the inner voice gets louder, telling him he's a faker and not good enough. Along the way he has racked up many amazing experiences, but Allan's inner voice is so loud it knocks all the wind out of his sails and he retreats into himself.

After a while he decided to give acting another go. In another astonishing demonstration of courage, Allan created a show in which he challenged himself with all the things he found most terrifying: solo performance, characterization through movement and audience interaction.

To make sure he didn't back out, Allan booked a tour of Canada. His performance attracted critical acclaim and he loved the energy of the tour, so the following year he decided to take it back on the road to a host of additional Canadian cities.

One night on tour, after the show, he checked his email to find a note from a guy named Marc-Andre, who was Casting Director at Cirque de Soleil. It was an invitation to audition for a clown position. Allan's first reaction was one of sheer excitement, followed by abject terror. The audition required him to do a two-minute clown piece, but he didn't have any ready. So he spent several hours constructing a detailed email listing all the reasons why he'd regretfully have to decline the best job offer of his life, and hit 'send'.

But Marc-Andre wasn't about to take 'no' for an answer. He turned up at Allan's show the following night and told him, 'You are exactly what we are looking for. Just do your thing.' The audition paid off and he was offered the role of The Giant Clown in Corteo. It was a massive career break.

From the outside Allan's story is a tale of one bold move after another. He dives in with great courage, prepared to be a beginner and learn on the job. He is dedicated to his craft and talented at what he does. He has been gifted many opportunities, not by luck, but because he puts himself out there. This is the story that I see. He is friendly and open, big-hearted and humble.

But that isn't the story that Allan sees. He talks of insecurity, fear, and depression, even after playing one of the greatest clown roles for the world's most famous circus. He is conscious of sabotaging his own success, and shares how he finds it hard to talk about his feelings and connect with other people.

He says he struggles to trust, and yet he is pouring out his story to me, a stranger introduced through a mutual friend. Where he talks of finding it hard to trust, I am moved by his openness. Where he sees failure, I am inspired by the foundations of a brilliant career. Where he calls himself an introvert who struggles to talk to people, I am wholly engaged, laughing out loud many times during our two-hour conversation.

The picture he paints of himself is not a portrait of the person I see before me. The story he tells is not the story that I hear, humming beneath the surface.

And so it is for many of us, who don't see the value in our own experiences, or recognize the potency of vulnerability.

Allan is working on a new series of storytelling workshops for people in business. He says he is finding it hard to reconcile the desire to share the whole truth of his journey with the need to be 'the expert' when teaching.

'How do I tell them about the failures without compromising my reputation?' he asks.

'What is the most important thing that you will teach?' I return.

'The value of being vulnerable,' he says, and then nods. 'Oh I see. I just answered my own question.'

Allan's example is a classic picture of a cage, right there. From his position inside it, he is trapping himself with a crushing lack of self-belief, seeing his growth as a series of failures. But from my position, outside of his cage looking in, I see the reverse. I see a man with unique experience and a beautiful humanity so deep and wide that it captured the attention of the world's greatest circus. I see a man with a wealth of experience, a huge amount to be proud of, even more to give, and a very bright future.

Do you see this in any of your friends? Do you know anyone who always puts themselves down? Do you see how what you see is often the exact opposite of what they see?

Now hold the mirror up to yourself in the same way, and look at yourself in reverse. What do others see in you that you can't see yourself? Where do you put yourself down, when others try to lift you up?

We would never judge a friend in the harsh way we often judge ourselves. We would never counsel them with the sharp words we reserve for self-coaching. And yet we all do it. We feed our fears and insecurities, and crush our own confidence.

Sometimes we manage to flee the cage, but then allow our old stories to catch up with us, and weigh us down.

Don't confuse your stories with your one beautiful story – the true story of your real life.

Write your own story. Rewrite it. Change the ending.

Know that in any moment you have the power to do that. And in doing so, you will build your momentum for escape.

Entry 11: The story of your life

First, the old stories...

1. *What are the stories you tell about yourself?*

2. *What if you flipped each of these stories and presumed the opposite was true. What would you tell yourself then?*

3. *What are the stories others tell about you? Are they true? Were they ever true? What might be different if you asked people to stop telling those stories, in that way?*

And now, your real story...

4. *Where in the world has your life taken you so far (physical places)? Which of those places had the most impact on you and why?*

5. *Who have been the main characters in your story? Write a few words about the role they have each played.*

6. *What has been the greatest tragedy of your story so far?*

7. *And the greatest comedy?*

8. *What has been your proudest moment?*

9. *What's going to happen in the as-yet-unwritten chapters about how you eventually triumph? Remember, you are holding the pen.*

10. *Let's imagine this version of your story is going to be published as a book. In which section of the bookshop can we find it?*

11. *What will the book be called?*

12. *What will the blurb on the back cover say? Who will endorse it, and what will their quote be?*

THE WEIGHT OF WORRY

A long time ago I had a fleeting romance with a Colombian naval officer. He was tall and handsome in a pristine white uniform, with gold buttons that sparkled against his deeply tanned skin. It was as innocent as could be, a meeting of eyes across the deck of his ship, a secret kiss in the summer rain. The inevitability of parting just a few days later only made it more enchanting.

When the time came for the *SS Gloria* to embark, my sailor waved goodbye with a white handkerchief, from his station high up on the mast. I felt like I had stepped into a tragic poem and imagined tears in his chocolate-brown eyes. There were tears in mine. I never actually thought I'd hear from him again.

But then the letters began.

He wrote me long missives in broken English, pouring his heart out from far-off lands as his ship toured the world. They were sweet and beautiful, with their airmail stamps and exotic postmarks.

We were supposed to meet up in France. My parents warned me off and I listened. I never turned up, but had no way of telling him I wouldn't be there. He called, heartbroken. I had no experience of such passion. His next letter proposed marriage, offering me a home in Colombia. I was flattered but overwhelmed, and never saw him again.

But then, a couple of months ago, I had a dream about him. Curious about what he was up to 20 years on, I looked him up on Facebook – always a dangerous idea. It turned out he was married with a son, and looked happy in his pictures. I was happy for him. Then he posted a picture celebrating his son's 18th birthday, and I did the maths. His wife must have been pregnant at the exact time he was courting me. I was shocked at the weight of my disappointment in him and in myself. How could he do that? How could he string a young girl along like that, and treat the soon-to-be-mother of his son like that? And how could I have not seen it? Was I really that naive? I felt at once protective and despairing of my younger self.

I went about my business as usual, but these thoughts hung over me, hijacking my mood for days.

That was it; I'd have to ask him about it.

So I did. And he explained, sweet and gentle like before. He wasn't his son's biological father. He met his son's mother when the little boy was already 18 months old, after I had stopped returning his letters. And with that my faith was restored. I could be genuinely happy about reconnecting, and knowing that he had gone on to find his own happiness.

Afterwards I reflected on what had just happened. How had I allowed a supposition, one that wasn't even true, to control my emotions, thought patterns and energy level for days?

Whenever I catch myself weighed down like this, I ask myself three questions that really help me get past whatever is in the way. In my interpretation of the inspirational work of Byron Katie, I ask myself:

1. Is it real?

2. Is it necessarily as bad as I think?

3. Does it really matter?

If only I had applied that to my own situation at the very beginning, I could have saved myself days of worry. Let's take a look.

1. Is it real? *I have no idea. I'd better ask. When I did ask I found out that no, it wasn't real.*

2. Is it necessarily as bad as I think? *No, not necessarily. There are many versions of this story that could be true. But I'll never know until I find out the facts. And when I did ask I found out that no, it wasn't as bad as I thought.*

3. Does it really matter? *This is the only question that really matters. And no, it doesn't. We are just a tiny crossing on each other's histories. We have separate lives now, and the truth or untruth of that story makes no difference to where I am, here and now, in this moment of my life.*

If you answer these questions with complete honesty, the vast majority of worries are shown up for what they really are – conjecture and supposition, rather than fact. Even if you do find yourself answering 'yes' to all three questions, you'll likely only do that in response to one or two major concerns. As the other concerns fall away, you can focus your attention where it's really needed.

And if you're worried about someone else, try flipping the questions you ask yourself. Instead of fixating on: ' How can I fix this?' or 'How can I save them from their troubles?', ask yourself: 'How can I love them?' That simple yet powerful change of perspective can shift you from worry to compassionate action, and shift them from the desperate to the loved.

It's so easy to get caught up in the weight of our worries, and let the thoughts run riot in our heads, but this limits our potential to really soar.

Not only do your thoughts and worries have weight, they also have energy. My energy completely changed in the days that I was worrying about something that wasn't even true. Time and again we have to remind ourselves that we get to choose what we think about and where we focus our attention.

The thing about worry is it doesn't achieve anything. It doesn't solve any problems, or make the thing you are worrying about go away. All it does is screw you up, filling your head with mindless negative chatter, which gets in the way of dealing with the things that are actually real.

You have already done the hard work of escaping the cage. Now it is up to you to shrug off the weight of worry and embrace the freedom that comes with travelling light.

Entry -12: Travel light

Imagine standing on a ledge at the entrance to your cage. The door has swung wide open, and you are ready to embark on the adventure of your life. But the only way out is to fly, so you need to make yourself as light as you can. You are allowed to take a kitbag with you, but the lighter it is the higher you will fly.

Right now, your kitbag is heavy. It is full of all the things holding you back and weighing you down. Imagine each of them as a brick inside that bag. Open your bag and unpack those bricks. Toss them away, into the vastness below. You don't need them where you are going.

Name each one as you take it out of your kitbag, and ask yourself those three questions:

1. *Is it real?*

2. *Is it necessarily as bad as I think?*

3. *Does it really matter?*

Once you have emptied your bag, think about what positive things you might like to take with you (and don't forget to pack that keyring with the Freedom Keys on it – you never know when you may need them again).

> **Note:** If you have answered 'yes' to all three questions and still have something weighing you down, check whether the worry is about someone else or yourself. If it's about someone else, ask, 'How can I love them through this?' If it's about yourself, ask, 'How can I love myself through this?'

Worry as a sign of compassion

If you have been a worrier all your life, it's a sign that you are kind and thoughtful, with a deep humanity and sensitivity. But expressing that compassion through worry is exhausting and fruitless.

If, instead, you can channel it as empathy, you can communicate your caring to whoever is suffering, without taking on the weight of their issues yourself.

It's the same if you are the subject of your own worries. Try being empathetic with yourself, treating yourself as you would a dear friend. Listen, try to understand what's at the heart of the issue, and be gentle on yourself. Show yourself you care. Be kind. Give yourself a bunch of flowers. Make some tea. Write yourself a thoughtful note.

This is a very different response to just worrying about your situation, and you'll find it much more nurturing and beneficial.

Entry -13: Worry release

Finding it hard to let go of some of your worries? Try this simple worry-release technique. It can give your mind some valuable respite, and raise your energy levels to a point where you can process things better.

Think back to a delicious memory and pinpoint some music that was playing at the time.

For me there are several songs that completely transport me: David Gray's *Please Forgive Me* has me crunching snow in the Italian Alps, watching my breath crystallize in the cold mountain air; Barbara Dickson's *Caravan Song* takes me to Tripoli, where the air is filled with the scent of frangipani blossom and freshly baked caraway seed bread; Michael Bublé's *Everything* takes me dancing on a favourite early date with Mr K.

Go multisensory. Tune in to the music but also smell the air, notice the colours, taste the experience. With practice you can disappear deeply into this in seconds, and switch out of worry mode any time you need to.

LETTING GO

A few years ago Mr K felt restless. He was frustrated in his career as a civil engineer, finding that the higher he went up the ladder, the more bureaucracy and politics he had to deal with. He needed a break after a decade at the same place. So we decided to take a six-month sabbatical in Kyoto, Japan. I hadn't been back in a while, and Mr K was keen to learn the language so he could talk to my Japanese friends.

We hatched a plan and went out in the spring of 2012. He went to school and I spent most of my time cycling round taking photos, learning how to make *washi* paper and discovering that I wasn't patient enough to be a weaver. It was a very special time.

We had no TV, no car, no phone. Besides the rent and school fees, Mr K was living on a budget of £10 a day, not much in one of the most expensive countries in the world. And yet I had never seen him happier. He ran every day, spent a lot of time by the river scribbling in his journal, and started drawing again for the first time since he was ten.

It was tough in the beginning when he didn't speak Japanese and had to ask me to order his dinner, but his hard work paid off and soon he was chatting to the locals and scoring top marks in his *kanji* tests.

Tucked behind a bakery off Horikawa Street, our whole apartment was smaller than our kitchen back home. The furniture consisted of one small dining table, two chairs, two desks, a bed, a small fridge, a one-ring hob and a rice cooker. If I put my arms out in the bathroom I could touch both walls at once, and only fitted into the cube-shaped bath if I hugged my knees to my chest. Not that I took many baths in the stifling heat of that Kyoto summer. A cool shower was much more appealing.

Anyway, it didn't matter because we had only brought one rucksack each for our six-month stay, having put all our belongings in storage back home. We decorated the place with local things – a sheet of handmade paper on one wall, a piece of fabric from a local temple on another. There was a place for everything, and room besides. There is no doubt that our minds were clearer and we felt lighter not being surrounded by stuff. And living in such a small space gave us ample reason to get outside every single day, even in the torrential downpours of the rainy season.

I have no doubt that all of this was a major part of the decision Mr K made when we were in Japan, to quit his career so we could work together at Do What You Love. He says it's one of the best decisions he has ever made.

～

Possessions can be a huge weight. Choosing to declutter, and selling or giving away things you no longer care for, can have a major impact on how you feel.

The hidden beauty of decluttering your physical environment is the mental space and emotional lightness it creates. There is a subconscious parallel between letting go of physical items you don't need, and letting go of negative thought patterns, blame stories and other emotional issues that clutter up your mind. It makes room for new possibilities, people and ideas.

Try it. It might surprise you.

Entry 14: Have a clear out

Go through each room of your house in turn, and look at every object. Ask yourself if you really need it, or if it makes you happy. If the answer is 'yes', keep it.

If not, do one of the following:

- *Sell it.*
- *Give it away.*
- *Recycle it.*

If this feels like too much of a mountain to climb, tackle one room at a time or one corner at a time. Even one object a day makes a difference.

Take stock of what you've released and see how you feel. Make a note in your journal about how different you feel afterwards. What else would you like to let go of?

THE UPLIFTING POWER OF FORGIVENESS

For a long time I really struggled with the concept of forgiveness. I would hear about people who had suffered atrocities 'forgiving' the perpetrator, and simply could not understand what it meant. Perhaps they were just a better person than me, being able to give a gift to the one person who had caused them such pain. But in time I realized, it's not about the other person at all.

Forgiveness is not about reconciliation with the offender or condoning what they have done. It is simply letting go of your response to an action against you. It is a declaration that you are not going to allow yourself to be weighed down by the impact of what someone else has done. It is a gift to yourself. It is grace.

Letting go of the desire for revenge or anger, or any other heavy response, isn't easy. But if you can find a way to forgive, you will find yourself lighter and uplifted.

Forgiving yourself is important too. For not doing the things you think you should have done, for having done the things you shouldn't have, for making mistakes, for not being perfect. All those things are part of being human and all we can do is to do our best, learn, grow and love.

LIFT YOURSELF

At any moment you have the strength and power to lift yourself. With your attitude and mindset and self-encouragement, you can be all the lift you need. If you can talk yourself out of something, you can talk yourself into it. If you have enough energy and attention to squash your own dreams, you have enough energy and attention to make them happen. You just need to redirect your energy and be kind to yourself. Self-confidence comes from telling yourself a different story. You are a beautiful bird. You were born to fly. It's up to you to start believing it.

We are often scared of our dreams, especially when they start coming true. We have to start talking about them and that's terrifying. We are scared of how big they are; of the changes we might need to go through to make them a reality; of whether they're right for us; of choosing just one thing (in case it is the wrong thing, because every choice has a consequence); that we won't have enough time, or money or willpower to see it through; of failure – or even success. But we'll never know unless we try. And when we try and things start to work, we start to trust and believe in ourselves a little more.

Sometimes we have to do drastic things to shake off the weight, to drown out the inner critic and find the inner strength to lift ourselves. But we must do whatever it takes.

To come alive, we must grow. And to grow, we must be courageous.

Focusing on the task at hand can help. When I was afraid to call myself a writer, I stopped thinking about it and just wrote. In time all the formal bits of it fell into place, while I kept focusing on doing the job. Writing the words. Taking the steps. Beating my wings.

To live the biggest, best and happiest life we can, we have to identify our dreams, and then chase them across the skies. Simple as that.

Courage lies in the making the choices that feel right for us. It doesn't matter if anyone else thinks it's brave. The word 'courage' comes from the Latin word *cor*, meaning 'heart'. You know in your heart what courage means to you. You know which is the courageous choice and when you've made it.

Remember, when courage is absent, the ego keeps on winning. But when courage is present, the soul wins every time. So summon that courage, and live from your brave heart.

We are so strong, but we often hide our strengths to fit in or keep the peace. Not anymore. Flying is hard work. It needs every ounce of strength that you have, so get clear on what you can offer and start building those flight muscles.

Entry 15: Your secret weapons

Acknowledging your strengths can provide armoury in the form of self-belief, self-knowledge, self-awareness and self-confidence.

First answer these questions as honestly as you can (now is not the time for modesty):

1. *How would a friend or close colleague describe you?*

2. *What have you done that others have complimented you on, or sincerely thanked you for?*

3. *In what kind of situations do you feel you react positively?*

4. *What kind of activities do you feel really engaged with when you are doing them?*

5. *What gives you energy?*

6. *What challenges do you enjoy?*

7. *What comes easily to you?*

8. *What qualities have helped you deal with fear in the past?*

Now look at your responses and see if there are any patterns coming up.

What strengths stand out? Strengths can usually be identified as the words following 'I am good at...' For example, things like communicating, planning, networking, inspiring others, having big ideas, making things happen, making other people feel good about themselves, etc.

Stick a photo of yourself in the middle of a page in your journal and draw spokes coming out from it, like sunshine.

If you prefer, you can download a template for this from www.bethkempton.com/flyfree.

In the gaps, write your top six to eight strengths.

This is your armoury of secret weapons. Use it well. Go back to the bird you drew for Entry 9 (see page 133) and make sure all these strengths are listed next to the upward 'lift' arrow, as truths that your inner sage tells you.

Horizontal forces: Drag + Thrust

Those around us can tread on our dreams or help us build them. The impact we let them have on us depends on three things:

1. The nature of their love.

2. The angle of their intention.

3. Our ability to deflect or absorb the energy they give out, depending on what serves us best.

People can have a negative impact on your confidence, convictions and actions. This 'drag' holds you back, making you do what you think you should, based on what they say. If you're always looking over your shoulder you cannot see ahead.

But others can also have a positive impact on your confidence, convictions and actions. This 'thrust' catapults you forward, strengthening your belief, encouraging you to fly higher. It is a positive wind beneath your wings.

THE INCONVENIENCE OF AUTHENTICITY

As you seek freedom and take steps towards doing what you really love, you will have to make many choices. It is inevitable that some of those choices will not work for everyone. Some people may find them inconvenient, or threatening. Others simply won't understand them.

But guess what? That's their problem.

The hopeful voices in your heart are telling you something important – don't let the naysayers drown them out.

When you go through any kind of deep change, particularly in mid-life when those around you think they have you figured out, it can be incredibly scary. When you are going through it, there are many things that you won't understand either, so you can be sure most others aren't going to understand, especially if you can't communicate what is happening. And when you emerge out the other side, you will have a different perspective on life. Perhaps you will be unwilling to play the same role in friendships, to do the same work, to accept the same treatment. You won't want the same conversations or be satisfied with the same old routine. You will realize you are seeking different things now. Know that this will be challenging, for you and for others.

Everyone has to get used to this version of you, but some people won't like it. They might not recognize you or, even if they do, they might not relate to you so well. Or perhaps your brave metamorphosis shines a light on their craving for a different way of living, and that will be truly uncomfortable.

It is often those closest to us that hold us back, but we have to find a way around that, to bring them on board with our dreams, or at least help them understand so they don't continue to stand in the way.

The closer someone is to you, the more likely they are to be affected by the changes you are making. Some people will actually sense your growth, and want a piece of it. Often they will react by trying to hold on more tightly, rather than giving you room to spread your wings.

> *Pay close attention to how you feel around certain people. Tune in to who is dragging you down, and try to understand why.*

Perhaps they feel threatened, or afraid, worried they won't be able to relate to you any more. If this is the case, it's time for a real heart-to-heart. Who knows? They might surprise you with their support. If you can talk them round you might find a great new ally.

But if not, consider distancing yourself, even just for a while, so you can recalibrate and test out your wings. Taking flight is a delicate and sometimes dangerous thing, which requires a clear head and a committed heart.

Just because they're family or your oldest friend, doesn't make them right.

Just because you've always listened to them, or given in to them, doesn't mean you have to keep on doing so.

Just because they've always done things a certain way, followed a certain career path, or made certain choices, doesn't mean that's the right road for you too.

Becoming your true self may be testing for you and inconvenient for other people, but ultimately, you will be happier if you make the choices that allow you to do what you love. And if you're happier, your positive energy will ultimately have a ripple effect on others.

Don't be afraid to go after your dreams, regardless of what anyone says. Remember, this is your life we are talking about. YOUR life. Your LIFE.

Entry 16: Drag + Thrust

Go back to the bird you drew in Entry 9 (see page 133).

Alongside the arrow pointing backward, away from the direction of flight, list everything others tell you that is still holding you back, even though you have already made the major step of escaping your cage.

Alongside the arrow pointing forward, list the ways in which other people thrust you forward. Take a moment to be grateful for them.

> Look carefully at your bird and the opposing forces. How can you reduce the drag and increase the thrust? How can you lose some of the weight and increase the lift?
>
> Try it, and report back to your journal.

BREAKING FREE

In researching this book I reached out to my online community, and hundreds of people bravely responded with their stories of incarceration and escape. One of the questions I asked was about who was affected by their being trapped. Their answers both buoyed my heart and crushed it. Of those who were married or had long-term partners, their responses fell into three categories:

1. My partner is amazing.

2. My partner is supportive but doesn't really get it.

3. My partner is the problem.

I send a silent prayer of thanks to all those partners who are there when their loved ones are freaking out, depressed, anxious, sad, disillusioned or stuck, who try to help them through and love them more than ever. Mr K is one of them, and I am truly grateful to him.

For those who are supportive but don't get it, I hope find stories in these pages which help you get through to them, because sometimes it's just a matter of understanding, or finding the right words. Who knows, they may even feel trapped themselves, and this could be an opportunity for you to help each other.

But for those who see their partner as the issue, for those who are in a toxic, even abusive, relationship, I send you a giant hug, and wish you safety. Love is so intoxicating that it is easy to get hooked on other people. We want to impress them, engage them, make them happy. Sometimes we meet the right people at the wrong time. Sometimes we make the best of people who used to be right for us. Sometimes we just end up with the wrong people.

Anyone wielding power and poison is not offering real love. It is often only once we have escaped a cage like this that we can see just how dangerous that cage really was. One brave woman who has done just that is Susan Hunter, whose name I have changed for privacy.

∼ Trapped in a relationship ∼

Susan was trapped in a toxic, controlling relationship for many years. Her husband's abusive language soaked deep into her psyche and her self-esteem sunk low. She was in poor health, had no energy and felt held back from doing anything she loved. It took her many years to realize that he wasn't going to change and it wasn't healthy for anyone, not least her children.

Having recognized her cage, she let go of her fear about speaking out, and in so doing found the confidence to leave him. Susan and her children were homeless for a while, and harassed and threatened by her husband, so they had to move across the country with very little money. Life was hard. But every time Susan felt anxious about what might become of them, she reminded herself that she never wanted to return to that cage. When things got really tough she looked to her friends for support, and found her free self returning.

Having spent years focusing on her children, she is now doing what she loves, teaching art to children and adults. Her grown children see those difficult years as a time where they were strong and looked after each other, and are hugely proud of their mother.

It's better to be free to be yourself than trapped by the controlling 'love' of the wrong person. It's completely possible that by living trapped, you haven't been your true self with your partner for some time. It might simply be a matter of telling them what's really going on, and asking them to be there, as you explore the road ahead.

But if you talk with openness and honesty, and still cannot get through, then maybe it's time to consider whether being together is really serving you both. Perhaps there has been a lesson in your relationship, which you can be grateful for. Love always gifts us something. It is never a complete waste of time or energy. But it also doesn't have to be forever.

In seeking freedom you need to look at every nook and cranny of your life to find out what is holding you back, then find a way to deal with it, improve it or leave it behind.

LEAVING OLD LOVES BEHIND

What about when we are held back by a love that left long ago? When we still care about what they think, even if they are no longer watching? My first true love broke my heart and I allowed the pain to drag me down for years, until finally I realized what was going on and broke free. Had I never met him, my story would have been poorer, so I want to share it with you because it shows how there is good in everything, how the pain can be fuel for growth and learning can be so precious.

$$\sim\!\!\!\!\sim\!\!\!\!\!>$$

My first love was a free-spirited hippie child. Let's call him The Boy. He grew up in a lighthouse, burned incense and somehow made life seem full of mystery.

When we finally got together one summer I didn't quite believe it. We were an unlikely pair. The first time he kissed me in the darkness of my parents' garden, I thought there was no sweeter kind of happiness.

I wanted to see the big wide world because of what The Boy told me about it. Even though he hadn't travelled far, he was an old soul wiser than his years.

He would send me letters from the rusty old camper van he lived in, written by the light of a candle, as he sipped whisky to keep warm. Then he moved to Scotland, and I went back to university, and our relationship was more in my head and my heart than in person, but I was still smitten. I planned the places we would go, the stories we would tell, the things we would discover together. I felt loved and happy, until he ran off with another girl, leaving me lost and alone.

To be fair to him, he had the decency to do the 250-mile round trip to tell me to my face that it was over. I shrunk into the corner of my room, stunned and shocked and eaten up. As I watched him go, I desperately wanted to follow, to beg him to stay, but I knew if I started to speak I would bleed with the pain. I followed him out to the car park and watched him climb into his camper van. His eyes were compelling me to say something, anything, but still I had no words. So he drove out of my life, and I fell to my knees, howling at the moon.

For months I felt physically sick if anyone mentioned The Boy's name. Time helped me heal and it's not like he haunted all my days. I loved life at university. But The Boy was always there, in the back of my mind.

The months turned into years. I graduated and headed back to Japan, this time to work. My older brother Jon, who had graduated a year earlier and hadn't yet figured out his next move, decided to come with me. He got a job as an English teacher, and by some good fortune was stationed just an hour away.

One summer evening we gathered with friends for an all-night party in a forest. Thirty of us congregated under a full moon, drinking Asahi and roasting chicken skewers. The sky fell black and the shadows closed in. Some of us were dancing. Faces flickered in the firelight. Spirits were high.

Then someone mentioned that Jenn could tell fortunes. I was a total sceptic, but ever curious, I wanted to try it.

Jenn looked at my left palm, then into my eyes, and said, 'Someone somewhere is doing something which on the surface is very painful for you. But in time you'll understand that it's the right thing. In time it will set you free.'

I had no idea palm reading could be so specific, but clearly she was onto something. My brother Jon, who had been listening over my shoulder, went as white as a sheet.

'What's wrong?' I asked.

He looked at me, at Jenn, then back to me again. 'The Boy is getting married today. And seeing as we're eight hours ahead of the UK, his bride probably just walked down the aisle.'

I couldn't breathe.

After that revelation, I went on to have many brilliant adventures and a few short-lived love affairs with lovely guys, but I hit 30 without any prospect of getting married or having children. I never quite managed to give my whole self to any man.

Part of me still compared each one to The Boy and of course they weren't him. And I never wanted to be the clingy girl, so I'd make a point of heading off to far corners of the world on my own, I guess in part to show I didn't 'need' them. I didn't realize that people need to be needed, and the right people want to be part of something with you.

I spent my 30th birthday alone, drinking G&Ts in a hammock on a beach north of Mumbai. As I looked out over the sea, I went through each year of my twenties, and raised a toast to all the good things that year had brought.

By the time I finished reflecting on my 29th year, I was on my tenth G&T and mesmerized by the lapping waves and setting sun. In that moment I knew I was ready to choose love as the greatest adventure of my thirties.

I recognized that The Boy had taught me much, set me off on a journey of discovery that would take me to every continent in the world, and given me a curiosity about cultures and religions and people that would never fade, but I also recognized that his life was no longer my life, and I needed to move forward. From then on I would be open to a love that would help me fly, not hold me back.

Within a few weeks of that day and that decision, I met Mr K. Suddenly I wanted to share all my plans and for us to make new ones together. I didn't want to travel alone, I wanted to share the quest and the stories and the creaky beds in spooky hotels with him. I wanted to share sunrises and moonrises and tales from the road, not over a drink when I got home, but right there, on the road, while it was happening. I fell in love in a completely new kind of way, with someone moulded from the same clay.

And then I realized The Boy hadn't been my destination. He was a way-pointer on the route. Not just any way-pointer, a deeply important, hard-to-forget way-pointer. Without his influence, I am not sure where I would be today, but it's unlikely I would have taken so many risks, and gone on so many adventures so soon. I realized I had needed him so I could follow where he pointed, but not to stay forever at the crossroads beside him. Looking back I like to think that maybe I had a role to play in his story too.

There are always people in our lives who play these roles, who we keep trying to please long after they have gone from our lives. All of this is drag, holding us back and hampering our flight.

Some people cross our paths on the way to somewhere else, some run ahead and encourage us forward, some travel with us for a while and then head off down some other path. But we aren't supposed to walk every step of the journey with every single person.

Remember, nothing is wasted. It's experience, and that is part of your growth and flight. Recognizing this can help you release the drag of those who no longer need to be in your life, and fly free.

POWER PEOPLE

The most effective way to be thrust forwards is to surround yourself with people who enhance your power, not diminish it. You can tell who belongs in which camp by the way they react when you explain your hopes, as well as how they react if you dare to share your fears. If you don't have this kind of support in your inner circle, fear not, we'll explore how to find it in the next chapter.

In Celtic tradition there is a beautiful concept called *Anam Cara*, which means 'soul friend'. It reflects the idea that our souls need love like our bodies need air, and this love can awaken new dimensions of ourselves. According to John O'Donohue in his beautiful book of the same name, an *Anam Cara* recognizes the real you without any pretence or disguise. Theirs is a deep spiritual friendship unaffected by geographical distance or time. Your *Anam Cara* understands you in a way that makes you feel you belong together, with your destinies intertwined. If you have an *Anam Cara*, take good care of that person, as they are precious indeed.

And if you don't have an *Anam Cara* right now, invite your free self to be yours. You have to practise self-love on an epic scale to feel truly free. You have to counter the negative voices in your head and hold your own hand through it all. In the end your free self is your greatest ally and truest friend. Treat them well and give them reasons to stay close.

Entry 17: Moving on up

Try to suspend judgement and do the following exercise as honestly as you can, building on what you listed on your bird diagram in Entry 9 (see page 133).

Take a fresh page in your journal and divide it into three columns. In the left-hand column write 'DRAG', in the middle column write 'NAME' and 'THRUST' in the right-hand column.

In the middle column make a list of the people you spend most of your time with. Leave some space between each name.

In the left-hand column, put a tick next to anyone who has a 'Drag' effect on your flight.

Next to each person whose negativity has a drag effect, write exactly HOW and WHY they might do it. Are they afraid? Threatened? Something else?

In the right-hand column, put a tick next to anyone who has a 'Thrust' effect on your flight. Next to each person who thrusts you forwards with their positivity, write exactly HOW and WHY they do that. This might be a good time to send them a quiet prayer of gratitude.

> **Note:** It's quite possible that some people may have both a drag and a thrust effect on you.

Now think about each person in turn:

1. *If they ONLY thrust you forwards, let them know how much you value their support, and see if you can spend more time around them in the coming days and weeks to keep you fired up at this crucial stage of your journey.*

2. *If they BOTH drag you backwards and thrust you forwards, think about how you could encourage them to do more of what they are doing when you feel supported. Let them know it is helping, and share the journey. Once you have opened up the conversation, find a way to help them understand why flying free is important to you, and show them how you need their support to lift you further. This can be a great opportunity to explore whether they feel trapped, and if so, how you can also help them to fly free.*

3. *If they ONLY drag you down, think about how you might help them understand why flying free is important to you. Give them a chance to support you and they might just surprise you. If you cannot think of any way to bring them round, or you try and it doesn't work, make a plan to distance yourself for a while. If it is someone you live with, try to get away by yourself for a few days. Even a small distance can make a big difference.*

4. *If you realize that the majority of the people you spend time with drag you backwards more than they thrust you forwards, it's time to look for a new community. (We will explore this in the next chapter.)*

Is there anyone no longer in your life that is having a drag effect on you? If so, acknowledge what they have taught you, thank them for it, and then let them go. Write them a letter and then burn it, meet up to talk and get closure, or just sit awhile and visualize yourself free of them. It is only you who is allowing them to remain in your life, hampering your flight.

> **Note:** If you are experiencing grief from the passing of someone you loved, this is a completely different situation. Besides seeking professional support if you need it, it can be valuable to consciously invite the person you have lost to be with you on this journey. Imagine how they would feel to know you are flying free, light and happy, with purpose and promise. Ask them to be there for you, in your heart, as you take flight.

BEWARE THE DOUBLE CAGE

When you have just escaped a cage, you are at your most vulnerable and at greatest risk of getting trapped again, by another cage. Once you are out of the cage, you no longer have the 'protection' of the bars, which is why emerging can be so hard. It's raw, forgotten, unfamiliar. This is exactly what happened to Sam Reynolds.

～ Supporting others like you ～

In 2005, aged 26, Sam had a glamorous job in film and her first diagnosis of breast cancer came as a huge shock. Treatment went well and she went back to work part-time. Her little girl, Lottie, was born in 2010 and life seemed to be getting back on track. But when Lottie was two, the cancer returned.

Yet again Sam went through treatment, and got the all clear the following year. A natural doer, Sam felt obliged to put her cancer experiences in a box and move on. And that is when the problems really began. Before long, Sam felt overwhelmed and alone, and was diagnosed with Post-Traumatic Stress Disorder (PTSD). Just a year later, aged 35, Sam was diagnosed with cancer for the third time. She believes the stress of the PTSD contributed to it. In the end she had a double mastectomy and got the all clear for the third time.

When she stepped out of the clinic for the final time she was determined to do things differently. Sam realized that she was no longer the same person and needed to find a new way to be in the world. She now wanted to help others avoid the high rates of depression and PTSD that so often follow cancer, and wanted to forge a new path.

Now Sam runs SamSpaces, which provides mentoring, support and events for people who are relearning how to live after cancer, as well as free meet-ups for cancer survivors around the UK.

Sam has been deeply moved by the experience of meeting and supporting others like her. She has learned that trying to shut out the truth of your experience actually consumes you, and traps you in another cage. But if you acknowledge it, talk about it, and respond with radical self-care, it doesn't have to be that way.

The fact is, sometimes the double cage happens. But remember, you now have all the tools you need to get out. With every experience of being trapped and breaking free, the less time you stay trapped, and the easier your escape.

NURTURE YOURSELF

If a mother bird is sick and exhausted, who is going to bring her babies juicy worms to eat? Taking care of herself is a huge part of taking care of her offspring. And so it is with us.

To soar we need to be fit and fed, stretched and rested. Martyring ourselves with little sleep, hastily made meals, extreme workloads, excessive commitments to others, mental stress and unnecessary worry serves no one. We need to take care of mind, body and soul, filling ourselves up with goodness so we can give goodness back.

If you already do this I bow down to you. If you don't, fear not my friend. You're not alone. Let's begin today.

Your energy is precious. The more you spend on things that don't make you feel free, the more drained you'll become. The more you spend on things that buoy your spirit, the higher you will fly.

Sometimes taking care of ourselves is all we need to do. And yet, time and again, it's the last thing we do. We all need to:

* Eat well.
* Drink water.
* Exercise.
* Pause and rest.
* Take time in nature.
* Take an active interest in our own health – before, during and after sickness.
* Be gentle on ourselves.
* Spend time in good company, making time to laugh and space to love.
* Make room to create beauty.
* Give ourselves permission to put ourselves first.

It's all so obvious and yet it so often goes by the wayside when things get busy.

Even though I know in my bones this is the truth, actually doing it is often hard. I know how important it is to slow down, to take time off and relax, but my natural response when things are challenging is simply to work harder and longer. I care for other people much better than I care for myself, so investing my energy in the right places – and making a conscious effort to recharge my batteries – is something I am always working on.

Every time I do take a proper break, whether it's half an hour to walk by the sea, a day at the spa or a week away with no phones or Internet, I always come back recharged, revitalized and ready for anything.

Every time we take care of ourselves, we renew our capacity for self-restoration. The more we do it, the easier it gets. We give ourselves the space to grow, and the energy to fly.

Nurturing yourself is vital for flight energy and stamina. It's the combination of physical and mental strength that allows you to soak into the experience of your life, eyes, mind and heart wide open.

THE JOY OF FLIGHT

So that's the theory over. You are now ready to leave your cage behind, and take flight. It may be a long time since you last took to the air. You may be anxious, or even terrified. That's normal.

Have faith, spread your wings and leap anyway. Because your free self is there to catch you, and lead you out into the vast world beyond the cage.

When you step off that ledge and into your life, everything you no longer need falls away and you are left with all that matters.

Chapter 12

CHOOSING YOUR DESTINATION: DECIDING WHERE TO FLY

It seems like a lifetime since I was lying, a shattered mess, on my bedroom floor, but it was actually just 15 months ago. Back then I couldn't have imagined writing a book before my new baby turned one. But I did it, by taking one small step after another, with the goal of feeling free.

As I have shared, the more space I made, the more seemed to open up, which eventually made room for this book. But remember, the book itself wasn't the destination. The destination was always 'feeling free'. In activating the Freedom Keys in pursuit of that feeling of freedom, I discovered a route that has lit me up every step of the way.

YOUR DESTINATION MATTERS

When you're trapped in the cage, anywhere would be better, but once you're out, your destination matters.

Doing what you love is awesome. It gives your work meaning, allows you to use your talents and fuels your creativity. And it's fun. But, actually, it's not the end goal. It's not the destination. The destination is feeling free, whatever that feels like to you. Doing what you love is simply a great way of getting there.

When captive birds and animals are released into the wild, the highest survival rate is seen when a detailed reintroduction plan has been put in place. So we're going to build you a personal Flight Plan to give you the confidence to take flight.

NAVIGATING TO YOUR ESSENCE

By its very definition, navigation requires a destination. What if I told you that 'somewhere' doesn't have to be a physical place, doing a thing? How different might your Flight Plan look, if you navigated instead to your essence, where you feel free?

If you head off blindly with no thought for your direction of travel, the likelihood of you getting somewhere you want to go is slim indeed. It's for this reason that planning is a surprisingly important skill for the Freedom Seeker. This is planning of the soulful kind. It's taking an active role in directing the experience of your own life.

Your 'Flight Plan' is not a formal commitment set in stone. It's a scribbled map that you can fold up and stash away in your pocket, to be brought out when you need confirmation of the route, or to check your progress. Imagine it written with a well-worn short and stubby pencil, so you can rub bits out and add to it as you go.

If you have a plan, you can change it. But if you have no plan at all, you are lost before you begin. It's about avoiding a tyranny of choice, by getting clear on the things you want to choose between. The more you narrow it down, the less the actual choice matters, because you will be choosing one of several paths you could take towards that destination of feeling free.

I can see, looking back, how true this has been for me. There has clearly been a career thread of helping others achieve their potential, but I'm not sure I was aware of that at the time. Instead of chasing a particular profession or promotion or other socially recognized form of success, or doggedly pursuing one particular passion, I have instead always tried to make decisions that take me in the direction of feeling free.

At 17 'navigating to my essence' meant choosing a university course that would lead me to adventure.

At 21, degree in hand, it meant taking a job that would take me back to Japan for more adventure, lured by a fascination with Zen philosophy and the Japanese aesthetic. This included the opportunity to interpret for some of the world's top athletes at major events like the Winter Olympics and World Games, supporting them at their most crucial competition moments.

From there, it meant taking other jobs that would allow me to travel the world, discovering new cultures and ways of life, through work in the sports industry and with UNICEF.

In nearly every case someone took a chance on me, gave me a role beyond my capability and challenged me to grow into it. Only once did I take a job through a formal interview process. Every other opportunity was born out of the one that came before it.

At 30, it led me to Mr K, who would teach me that it's possible to feel free with someone else.

At 33, it led me to a creative awakening, which in turn led to starting my own business, innovating careers guidance and offering support for people wanting to live a more unconventional life.

At 36, it led me to becoming a mother for the first time, to Sienna.

At 38, it led me to realizing the need to carve out space, at the same time as I became a mother for the second time, to Maia, and then to writing this book.

One different decision at any point would have sent me in a different direction, and all the subsequent paths would also have been different. But I am sure there would have been other paths, because I was always making decisions based on the same rationale – the desire to feel free.

The benefits of this are manifold:

* There are no mistakes, just different paths. Nothing is wasted as it leads you to another path.

* You can always change the path.

* You don't need to know the route, just where you are navigating towards. You can simply make one navigational choice after another, and this becomes your route.

❀ The route matters a lot less than you might think. Society makes it all about the route and the trophies you collect along the way, but there are infinite routes to your essence and that is the only destination that really matters.

❀ There's no time limit for starting or finishing, so it's never too late. But the experience is life so the sooner you wake up to it the richer that will be.

❀ Planning is good. Spontaneity is good.

❀ Travelling with friends is good. Meeting new friends on the way is good.

❀ Feeling the ups is good. Feeling the downs is good.

❀ It's all good because it's all leading you to your essence – the place where you feel free.

When I look at the connected dots with the benefit of hindsight, some parts of my journey seem unlikely, fantastical even. But at the time I usually just chose the next most interesting, most exciting thing that would make me feel free.

It's vitally important that you make choices as you go. Not choosing is a choice in itself – a choice to give away the power to determine your own flight path.

Of course every choice has a consequence, and choosing one thing equates to not choosing others. That can be scary, to the point that many of us suffer from 'FOMO' (Fear of Missing Out). This results in either not making a choice at all, or rushing around trying to do everything and burning out. A friend of mine, Kate Eckman, brilliantly reframed this when she said, 'From now on I'm opting for JOMO instead – the Joy of Missing Out.' I love this. It's far healthier and allows us to soak into the experience of the choices we've made, rather than wasting energy and attention on the things we didn't choose.

A new destination means uncharted territory. That means you get to be an explorer of this final frontier. Making choices prevents life becoming something that happens to you, and instead makes it something you map out for yourself.

You see, for Freedom Seekers, feeling free is the whole point.

As soon as you realize that your quest is to feel free, you start to navigate your life in a completely different way.

Remember, we have defined freedom as 'the willingness and ability to choose your own path and experience your life as your true self'. That, my friend, is how you really come alive.

CHOOSING YOUR WAY THERE

Your eight Freedom Keys are not just the way out of your cage. They are also a manifestation of what 'feeling free' means to you in the long term. The difference is that when you use your Freedom Keys in 'unlocking mode', they are likely to be a temporary solution, whereas when they are used in 'flight mode', as ongoing life guidance, they become a long-term solution. Your Freedom Keys are therefore vital for building your Flight Plan.

The experience of escaping the cage may have already given you some clues about what you'd like to 'do'. You might have thoughts about a new career path, starting your own business, teaching perhaps. Or a new way to organize your days, work more flexibly, carve out more time for the things you love.

Even if you think you know what you want to do, sometimes you may have to change your mind along the way. If you are completely focused on one particular job or opportunity and it doesn't work out, it's easy to slip into beating-yourself-up mode. But if you simply navigate towards a feeling of freedom, then changing the route you take to get there won't feel like a failure at all.

In the end, if you feel free and embrace the experience of flight, then what you actually did to get there matters a whole lot less than you might think.

So stay open, and see what emerges.

Entry 18: What is calling you?

Go back to the Freedom Keys (see pages 45–119) and choose the one calling to you most right now. Write it on a sticky note or slip of paper and put it on the table in front of you.

Now look back at your responses to Entry 15: 'Your secret weapons' (see page 157). Write each of these on a sticky note or slip of paper. Put these in a circle around the note stating your chosen Freedom Key.

Move your eyes in and out from the centre of the circle to each piece of paper and back again, and see what connections start firing in your brain. In your notebook make a note of anything that springs to mind. It doesn't matter if it seems completely random. It might be a noun, a verb or an adjective. It doesn't matter if it's a job title, an industry, a person's name, a song or a place. It can be anything. Let your brain go wild.

If you were particularly drawn to a second Freedom Key, repeat the exercise with that one in the middle. Carry on adding to your list of connections. Try not to judge them. Repeat with as many Freedom Keys as you like.

Now look at your overall list of words and see what themes are starting to emerge. Draw lines between things that are connected. Make a note of what commonalities are jumping out at you. We will come back to them shortly.

DO WHAT YOU LOVE

Feeling free and doing what you love are intrinsically linked in a virtuous cycle. The more you do what you love, the more free you feel, and the more free you feel, the more capacity you have to do what you love.

For most of us, to truly fly free, we need to extricate ourselves from worries about paying the bills, and to do that we need to either simplify our lives or earn some kind of income. This is the beauty of doing what you love within your work. In some cases it's not so much about the work that you do, but the way you do it, and there have never been more options available to us.

The right choice

Mandy Henry was a full-time presenter for MUTV, Manchester United FC's sports channel. She loved her work, but found the shift pattern incompatible with her desire to travel. So Mandy went freelance in 2012 and has never looked back. She now takes three months a year off to travel and blog about her adventures, and spends the rest of the year presenting for MUTV, the BBC, Premier League TV and many high-profile events. She earns more than before, chooses the nature of the work she does and is deeply appreciative of the opportunities her work offers. And she feels so much freer.

Of course, in some cases the thing you are most passionate about may not be a viable career option, whichever way you approach it. In that case aim to set up your life in a way that gives you as much time as possible outside work to pursue what you love the most.

Sometimes when we start grappling with a question as large as 'What shall I do with my life?' we end up going round in circles. We need to stop getting caught up in the detail and start putting our imaginations to work.

When you have been trapped in a cage for a long time, it's natural to limit the scope of your dreams, but outside the cage your imagination is as vast as the sky.

Entry 19: Put your imagination to work

Imagine for a moment that everything in your life is taken care of – all the people who need you are fine and cared for, the bills are paid, you don't need to work and your time is your own. You have 12 months to do whatever you like. The only rule is that it has to be something that makes you feel free. How would you spend the year?

Try really hard not to put the usual restrictions on your ideas. Try not to be rigid in your thinking. This is the time to really dream. Allow your mind to wander and reach out to faraway possibilities (and seeming impossibilities).

In your notebook, write down as much detail about your vision as you can, or draw a picture of what you saw.

Make notes about how you felt in your vision. Besides feeling free, what kinds of feelings were layered beneath?

Now think about why this particular vision might have come to mind. What is it telling you? Think about how your vision connects to the themes you came up with in Entry 18: 'What is calling you?' (see page 183). That exercise will have put your subconscious to work, so this vision is no accident.

Even if the exact vision isn't possible (or even desirable) in your current context, perhaps a version of it is, and the picture is showing you a way to find joy today, while building for tomorrow.

Think about how this might translate into your daily life now, and what it might be pointing to in the future. How could you most effectively use your time, money, energy and attention to get to a place where you feel like that? How could you start reprioritizing and reallocating resources right now?

Look back at your vision and see what questions you could ask, to set yourself up for the kind of future you envisioned. There are small things we can do every single day, and more significant things we can do over the long term, by starting to reprioritize and allocate our resources in a different way, starting today.

❧

I tried this exercise recently and was blown away by the vitality and clarity of my vision. I was in a house in a beautiful part of the countryside, with big skies and rolling hills. The kitchen door was open and I could see the garden beyond. I had my apron on, and I had just brought in a pile of vegetables from the garden. An open box of fairy lights and a pile of homemade gifts suggested I was preparing for a gathering of friends. There was a stack of handwritten notes on the table. I realized I was penning my first cookbook. Perhaps my friends were going to be in it, tasting the food, like something out of *Kinfolk* magazine. Next to my manuscript was a stack of travel journals with sticky notes poking out from the pages, pointing to scribbled recipes I had gathered from around the world. Apparently I was back from recent travels. I looked happy and I felt free.

This vision sounds dreamy to me. It combines many of the things I love, and I'm excited to think that a version of this could be in my future one day. Even if the exact scenario doesn't play out, it's a great place to navigate towards.

Right now it reminds me to question whether I am laying the foundations for such a possibility in the choices I make each day. Am I prioritizing time to cook? Am I taking lessons from talented chefs? Am I learning how to grow my own vegetables, or at least growing herbs in my kitchen? Am I gathering friends to eat around my table? Am I taking care of my friendships now, to make sure I still have friends in years to come? (That's a serious question.) Am I setting myself up to be able to live in a farmhouse, even if the reality of that is several years away?

Note: If you are struggling to see a vision that feels right for you, and you need additional time and support to get clear on what doing what you love could mean for you, consider joining The Society of Freedom Seekers at www.bethkempton.com where you can get direct access to support from me and others, to help shape your dreams.

DRAW UP YOUR FLIGHT PLAN

Too much choice can be paralysing, so an idea of direction helps you narrow it down. The steps of your Flight Plan are about nudging yourself towards your destination, and recalibrating as you go. But remember, your Flight Plan is just a guide. It's not fixed in stone. Perhaps the most important thing is finding a route, which in itself is an experience to relish.

~ Making it happen ~

Jennifer Barclay had dreamed of living on a Greek island ever since she'd spent a year in Greece after university. But it remained a dream until she hit 40. After going through two break-ups in quick succession, she decided it was time to think about what she wanted from her life next. Greece was calling, but she didn't just drop everything and hop on the next flight to Athens.

First Jennifer got clear on what would allow her to live on a Greek island. She needed to earn money, and her editorial role in publishing offered the potential to do that remotely, so she thought through the practicalities and did her research.

She discovered an island that was wild and remote enough to fit her dream, yet offered affordable housing and a reliable Internet connection. Not wanting to lose the momentum of a career she'd carefully built over the years, Jennifer negotiated a fixed contract for several days a week with a former employer. That gave her the confidence she needed to make the leap, and the security of being able to pay her rent long enough to know if she could make it work as a life choice rather than just an extended holiday.

In time Jennifer would go completely freelance, start her own editing business and literary agency, and become fluent in Greek. Crucially, her new lifestyle gave her time to flex her creative muscles, and write books based on her life on the island. She would make new friends, become part of a community that fascinated her, and breathe in the delicious Greek air every single day.

As Jennifer built her Flight Plan, she first got clear on what feeling free meant to her, noted the practicalities that would make her dream work, and then committed to making it happen. Once she had made the move she explored things that interested her and adjusted her flight path as she went.

Entry 20: Build your Flight Plan

Think about the vision you had in Entry 19: 'Put your imagination to work' (see page 186). This is a work in progress, so feel free to play with that vision until it is something that you actually want to make happen, and travel towards.

If you share your daily life with someone, and this goal will mean major changes, share your vision with them. Be sure to do it when they are relaxed, and have time to listen. Let them know this is just the very beginning of an idea, and you understand it might be unsettling for them. Try to find a version that excites them too. If you know they are likely to give you a slew of reasons not to do it, find a friend to talk it through with first so you are prepared.

Consider your vision to be your main goal. Getting to any major goal can be overwhelming, but breaking it down can make it so much more achievable.

Think about several mini goals you need to achieve in order to reach that main goal. List each mini goal in the past tense as if it has already been achieved. Psychologically this is very powerful, as it increases your confidence in your ability to achieve it.

1. *Take your list of mini goals and write them out over several pages in your journal, with one at the top of each page.*

2. *Break each mini goal into smaller steps, listing these on the page, in the past tense as if they are already done.*

3. *Put a deadline next to each mini goal and put the steps in your diary, carving out time to actually do each one.*

> 4. *At the bottom of the page write a list of resources you might need in order to achieve this mini goal, and any ideas you have about how to access those resources.*
>
> And now, the most important part, commit to your own flight in writing. Capture your vision in a single sentence. Stick it on the wall. Turn it into a piece of artwork, a poem, or a song. Announce it to a friend or just tell it to yourself. However you commit, commit.
>
> Remember, it's OK to change your mind, but you need to head somewhere. Go with this for a while, and know you can always adjust the route later.

BEGIN TODAY

However far away your dream of freedom may seem right now, the most important thing you can do is to simply begin. Take a step, any step. If the time feels right for a major step then do it. But if you aren't quite ready, or think all you need is a few considered tweaks, then start small and take whatever steps you can.

Sometimes you need to say yes to move forward. And sometimes you need to say no. It's like the phases of the moon. Depending on your stage of growth, when you are expanding and exploring, yes is good. When you are refining and honing, no is often better. Yes or no. Just choose and move.

Chapter 13

BIRDS OF A FEATHER: FINDING YOUR FLOCK

You know, I used to think I was an extrovert. I like people, and I loved performing on stage when I was young. Parties were fun and I'd happily talk to strangers. But then I got older and wasn't so keen to be caught up in crowds. I had no desire to be the centre of attention, and I found large gatherings quite draining. As I paid more attention to my stress triggers, I realized I needed quiet time more and more. I clearly wasn't an extrovert after all.

Then it became trendy to come out as an introvert, so I tried that label on for a while, but it didn't fit either. I needed time and space away from the noise to recover, but my ideas would come to life in conversation.

So I looked for an alternative and I discovered that there is a middle way called an 'ambivert': a bit of extrovert, a bit of introvert, not really sure about either. From the moment I heard the word I didn't want to be one. It sounded like some kind of cleaning product and felt like a manufactured option to describe the space on the spectrum between extrovert and introvert. It didn't work for me.

I thought about when I am at my most energized and creative, fizzing with potential, and realized I come alive in small gatherings of kindred spirits: people who are both practical and spiritual, challenging and yielding, gentle and strong. People who are smart and funny, but not 'in your face'. People who listen and share, but don't try too hard. People who'd rather say nothing than talk about nothing, but come alive in real conversation. And I know I'm not alone.

So I invented a new label for myself: I'm a 'kindrovert', and I suspect you might be one too. Us kindroverts light up by connecting authentically. We are nourished by sharing our truth and stories with a quiet confidence when the vibe is right. This makes us great travellers, because our need for real connection makes us curious in foreign lands. We like to wander, we ask good questions and we really listen to the answers. We are interested in other people's ways of life, belief systems and stories, and find a way to connect regardless of language.

Some of us lack confidence initially, but can shine with the support of others. A few kind and genuine words in our direction can do wonders, and we can step into enormous power in the presence of fellow kindroverts.

We'd rather make no new friends than make new superficial ones. But when we put ourselves out there, we can make friends with our kind of people very quickly. We trust deeply and are eminently loyal. We soak up the moments and remember the details. Sound familiar?

I like it that 'kindrovert' has the word 'kind' in it, because kindness given and received is energizing too, especially when it is unexpected and given without expectation. Kindness is what I needed when I was struggling. It's what we all need when we're struggling. And it's the gift we can give even when we don't have any actual answers.

If you come alive in small gatherings of kindred spirits, then you, my friend, are a kindrovert.

What difference does it make to know you're a kindrovert? It allows you to stop putting pressure on yourself to be in big groups, or make new friends as soon as you find yourself in a new situation. And if you recognize it in yourself, you have a better chance of recognizing it in other people. Your kind of people.

I have met many fellow kindroverts on the road, and I think that's partly why I associate freedom with travel. Sometimes it's easier with people who don't know our history. Instead of assuming, they offer us the chance to tell a new story, the story of our free selves. And the more we tell that fresh, hopeful story, the more we believe it, and the closer to our free selves we feel.

When I took my solo trip to Costa Rica, in the space of just 11 days I met six different people that I would gladly invite into my home, or talk with long into the night. They included one Italian, four Americans and one Brit. I wasn't searching for new friends. I was actually there to be alone, to write, think, stretch my body and mind, and have an adventure by myself. These new friends arrived not because I was looking for them, but because I was looking for myself. The happiest meeting of all was on the way home.

Xavier Rudd's 'Follow The Sun' filled my ears as I waited on the runway at Nosara Airport. I reflected on my restorative stay in the jungle and watched a speck in the sky morph into a tiny Cessna plane, which eventually came to a juddering halt less than 15 metres away.

Normally when I fly I protect my time and space. I love the hours of quiet, with no mobile phone or other distractions, and often use the time to read or think or journal. I rarely talk. But this time I got chatting to my neighbour – a friendly-looking surfer-type – and by the time we landed, I felt like I had made a new friend. It turned out we both had eight hours before our connecting flights, so we decided to go for lunch together in a nearby town.

We shared stories and burritos, and the hours flew past. Before we knew it, it was time to head back to the airport. As we stood in the queue for airport security, he hinted that there was a deep dark story in his past. I was intrigued and wanted to hear it, but time was running out. Bags and passports checked, we looked for our departure gates. There were still 20 minutes until my plane was due to leave, and then 10 minutes for him to get to his gate.

It was almost inevitable that he would come with me, sit by the window as we watched the planes taking off, and spill one of the most extraordinary, heartbreaking, heart-warming stories I have ever heard. That story isn't mine to tell, but I am grateful it was shared.

When my flight was called we stood up and hugged. 'Thank you,' we both said. 'I'm so glad I met you. I know we will meet again.'

As I boarded my plane home after an extraordinary trip, I carried with me the glow of connection with kindred spirits, knowing that my world has become even brighter with new friends in it.

BIRDS OF A FEATHER

Here's my theory. The world is full of Freedom Seekers, quietly doing their thing in all corners of the world. Each of us is at a different place on our journey of escape and we may have different flight trajectories, but we can sense each other, need each other, and can fly higher when we flock together.

When you activate any of the Freedom Keys, there is the possibility of meeting birds of a feather, connecting on a deeper level and growing together.

~ Finding your flock ~

In this dark storm the fickle sea is a shape-shifter, now a pool of molten granite, now an ancient monster rising from the deep. She rumbles and rages, grasping blindly skyward with her giant liquid fingers. In the midst of it all is Sea Dragon, a 22-metre steel-hulled sailing vessel built for one of the longest, most demanding ocean races ever imagined. In port she is majestic. But in these seas she seems as small as a child's toy bobbing in the bath.

If you zoom in close you'll see 14 figures clinging to the boat. Gripping the ship's wheel is an athletic blonde woman, hair ragged with sea mist, face tight with concentration. Emily Penn hasn't eaten or slept properly in five days, and still the storm rages on. The lives of her all-female crew are in her hands and she has to get through this.

It is Emily's first ocean crossing as a professional skipper, and she is feeling the pressure with a novice crew. As she clutches the helm, feet spread wide for maximum stability in the wild conditions, Emily clocks the monster rising. A huge wave is advancing towards them from the starboard side and there is nothing she can do about it. Most of the crew members don't register the menace, but Emily can only brace herself for the inevitable.

Everything shifts into slow motion, and she tastes salt spray on her lips moments before the wave hits, savaging the deck and sweeping tons of cold seawater into the boat. Emily is waist-deep, and everyone else has gone flying.

There are flailing limbs everywhere, the crew awash in the dark remnants of the wave with the breath knocked out of them. Emily knows everyone is harnessed and clipped on, but it's still a relief when her headcount reaches 14.

As Sea Dragon steadies herself, the women shake off the salty water and cast their gaze about, unsure how to react.

Now all eyes are on Emily, faces imploring, 'Are we alive? Are we OK?'

Emily's insides are in knots and her mind is racing. 'What the hell am I doing here? What have I done?' But she sees the plea in the eyes of her amateur crew and reacts the only way she can. Emily forces a grin and pumps the air with her fist and screams 'Woo hoo!'

The other women see their young skipper's reaction and instead of panicking, let out a collective call of whooping and cheering, proud that they have made it through the monster wave.

As one of the crew members challenges the ocean to 'Bring it on!' the bond between those 14 women is forever sealed.

Emily was 27 at the time. She is a skipper, ocean advocate and artist dedicated to studying environments in the remotest parts of the world. She is an international public speaker and advisor on issues relating to the ocean, our planet and the future of society, so she is no stranger to pressure. But this was different. It would become a defining moment for the scope of Emily's belief in what is possible when a small group of friends – in this case women – join hands to raise their collective spirits and work together.

As an experienced expedition leader Emily had sailed countless trips and encountered many storms, but this inaugural all-women 'eXXpedition' stands out in her mind.

'There was magic in the air,' she recalls. Although she was the leader from a technical and safety perspective, there was no tangible divide between paid skipper and paying crew. From a fish biologist to a product designer, from a filmmaker to an engineer, the women had all answered the same call to adventure, inspired by the expedition's mission to 'make the unseen seen, from the toxics in our bodies to the toxics in our seas'. They were on a shared quest for meaning, and had to work together to stay alive.

After that baptism of fire, they continued for the rest of the month-long voyage sharing stories, challenges, knowledge, laughter and real conversation. Their lives were forever changed by their shared experience, and they have gone on to make films, educate on ocean plastics, and run spin-off events for hundreds more women.

But perhaps even more importantly they are still friends, providing a constant source of love and support for each other regardless of their geographical distance. And it all started with that one gathering of a small flock of kindred seabirds, seeking freedom and finding each other.

OLD FRIENDS, NEW FRIENDS

Your flock – your community or tribe – is probably different to your long-standing circle of friends. Although both offer friendship, they play very different roles in your life.

You don't need to discard your old friends to make space for the new ones. Old friends can be a real blessing if you are trying to remember who you used to be, and if they truly want the best for you.

But if you are trying to escape from an old version of you, letting go of old stories and blossoming into something else, then old friends can hold you back. Sometimes it's more convenient or comfortable for them if you stay the same. They may love you dearly but try to clip your wings, ostensibly so you don't stumble, but actually so you don't fly the nest. If that is the case then you have a choice to make.

You can try to take them on the journey with you, or you can leave them behind, even just for a while, so you can settle into your new shape. It's worth talking to them about how you are feeling, because they may well surprise you. We all want to be seen; they may even open up about their own desire for escape.

There will be some people who fall into both groups – close friends who are also part of your flock. These people are truly a gift, and by recognizing each other as Freedom Seekers you can share the most amazing journey of growth and discovery.

Entry 2-1: My kind of people

Take a moment to think about the kind of people who would be 'birds of a feather' to you:

1. I want to spend more time with people who...

2. And who don't...

3. I want to spend less time with people who...

4. And who don't...

5. The people in my life who are already birds of a feather to me include:

6. When I think about the possibility of meeting more kindred spirits I feel...

Remember, when you start taking action in the direction of feeling free, you'll find fellow Freedom Seekers already there.

MIGRATING TOGETHER

There is an incredible power in Freedom Seekers uniting, in vulnerability and openness, with hope and determination. When we come together to support and celebrate one another, we build each other's confidence and everyone moves forward.

Birds of a feather don't just flock together – they also migrate together.

Support has been a crucial part of escape for all the Freedom Seekers in this book, and it works both ways. The more deeply you connect with others, the higher you will all fly.

~ Sisterhood ~

Deep in the Welsh countryside an old tin barn is being prepared for a very special gathering. Evergreen boughs and foraged flowers tumble over two long dining tables. Candlelight, refracted in vintage glass tableware, casts a soft glow across the room. Simple place settings of white linen and eucalyptus await guests. The wooden table, polished to a high shine by generations of rested elbows, hints at tales told and secrets shared across the years. This is a place for feasting and friendship, connecting and conversation, wishing and wonder.

The air is filled with the delicious hum of last-minute preparations and the gentle chatter of women gathered outside. When the barn doors are finally drawn back a collective gasp spills into the night. Members of the sisterhood take their places and the feast begins.

'It sounds like we're a witches' coven!' says Lou Archell, creator of Sisterhood Camp, as she describes the event to me. But then, when you consider the healing effect of the weekend, the reverence and ritual, the soulful transformations that happen under a full moon, perhaps she's closer to the truth than she realizes. A lifestyle and travel blogger by day, Lou created the

event to nurture her own need for women's company. She spends much of her day feasting her eyes on visuals online, but needed that offline connection with others who understand the value of quiet beauty and the importance of making things with your hands as a route to nurturing yourself.

The women attending the camp take workshops in natural flower arranging, ceramic pot-making, beach cooking, pebble art and more. But the deeper work goes on beneath the surface, as the hands mould clay, select stems, and paint stones.

Most of the gathered women are mothers, with busy jobs and hectic lives, but each finds a way to get there, even if it means sacrificing other things to pay for this experience. They arrange childcare to allow for self-care. And they leave energized, nurtured and deeply inspired.

Retreats like the Sisterhood Camp are more than the sum of their parts. Somehow the heady combination of feasting, fire and friendship leaves a shimmering magic hovering on the shoulders of participants as they leave the sanctuary of the experience. Although it fades with time, that feeling can still be accessed in the recesses of memory, with the stimulation of the senses. The scent of a peony, the steam rising off a china cup of chamomile tea, the rustle of leaves... Small things take us back there, but only if we have been there before, gathered together.

Freedom Seekers flock for warmth, helping each other through tough times and bonding over shared experiences, mistakes, parenting tips, jokes, worries, reading recommendations, recipes, cake and wine. We nourish each other with stories, compassion and love, and build trust and understanding.

∼ In the pursuit of motherhood ∼

Jessica Hepburn and her partner were desperate to have a baby but, after many years and over £100,000 spent on IVF, two years ago she finally gave up on giving birth to her own child.

Jessica largely travelled this hard road in silence. As one of the youngest chief executives in British theatre, she felt unable to share her journey with colleagues. While her friends knew what she was going through, they really couldn't empathize, having not been through it themselves. In the end Jessica shut everyone out, even splitting from her partner for a while, as the struggle became a wall between them.

Instead Jessica documented her story in The Pursuit of Motherhood, *the book she couldn't find when she needed it – an emotionally honest account of the secrecy, depression and pain that often surrounds infertility. She wanted to acknowledge that, however hard you try, there might not be a happy ending, at least not the one you are looking for, but that even out of so much disappointment can come opportunity and even triumph.*

The response to her book was so overwhelming that Jessica founded Fertility Fest, the UK's first ever arts festival on fertility, infertility and IVF. The festival attracted people from all walks of life, who may never otherwise have met, and yet were united by the theme of the day. Stories were shared, tears shed, friendships ignited, and everyone went home feeling a little less alone than before.

Although Jessica herself is still undecided about whether she will pursue motherhood through alternative routes, she has taken one incredible gift from the painful journey of the past few years, feeling the full force of humanity in the sharing of stories with others who have experienced the same thing.

There is also safety in numbers. The collective voices of many Freedom Seekers are more likely to be heard than lone voices, and as a group we have access to many more resources.

Keeping in regular communication with your flock is important for you and for your kindreds. Stay interested, stay in touch. Send love notes, reminding each other why you appreciate each other so much. Meet up if you can. Champion each other.

AGE IS BUT A NUMBER

The ages of the Freedom Seekers in this book span half a century, from those in their twenties to those in their seventies, while I'm somewhere in the middle. When we are young we tend to spend our time with our peers – at school, at university, on a graduate programme – and it is important to have friends at the same life stage as us. But one of the most precious things I have learned in all my freedom seeking so far is the beauty of friendships that cross age borders. We have something to give, and something to receive, whatever age we are.

~ Biker chick ~

Karen Walklin was a mental health nurse for 35 years before retiring a few years ago, aged 55. At first she felt thrilled and grateful to be retired, as she had longed for this time to follow her dreams of travel and creativity. But she had no idea how hard retirement would actually be. Karen moved house and suddenly found herself in a new area, without the routine of a job to go to every day. Her former colleagues were, of course, still at work and her friends outside work were scattered across the country.

It was at this time that Karen joined my Do What You Love e-course, and started to think more about her new direction. So often we associate the phrase 'do what you love' with work, but it only became something of a mantra for Karen after she had retired. It has now become her life philosophy, and her most precious decision-making tool. It has helped her find the gifts in her retirement and ensure her life right now is spent doing what she truly loves: being with her granddaughter, developing her art practice and riding her beloved motorbike.

Karen bought her first motorbike for £10 nearly four decades ago, to commute to work. She became totally hooked, and the biking became a passion, offering adventure away from daily routines. But it's only since retiring that she has been able to dive deeper, to combine her bike love with longed-for travel experiences further afield.

When I spoke to Karen, she was just about to ride her Ducati Monster 821 across Europe with her husband and a group of biker friends. I asked her what it feels like to be on the road.

'It's a great sense of freedom – just me and my bike. I can immerse myself in the whole experience: pure focus and concentration. I hear the wind and the sound of the bike, and soak in the sights, sounds and smells of the places I travel to. Even short rides are adventures as each is a new challenge. I think at times it's the closest I can get to feeling like a bird in flight. It can be so graceful too, almost like dancing. I am completely in the present, paying constant attention. It's like a meditation.'

In my eyes Karen is a rock star. I love the way that she pulled herself through the challenging time straight after retiring, and she has this advice to others in the same situation.

> 'Take time to think about who you truly are, and how you want to approach your newfound freedom so you can really live. It may be that you need to prepare and plan. It may be that you need to just relax and go with the flow. Whatever the case, hang onto your dreams, don't let them go, because they are going to lift you up. But be patient if things don't seem to be working out, because change takes time.'

People of different ages have different kinds of wisdom, different perspectives, different energy levels, different stories to share. We can all be generous with our friendship. Some people might bring you a fresh energy or hopefulness or just the savvy you need. Others might bring you a gentle calm, mothering warmth or wealth of fatherly experience. And it might surprise you who brings what.

You have something important to offer, however old you are. Think about what that is, and find a way to share it with other Freedom Seekers.

Entry 22: Try flockworking

Choose one idea from the list below, or come up with your own, and commit to putting yourself out there where your flock may be. Decide on at least one action you can take right now to take it forward:

1. *Think back to your Freedom Keys, then think about places that people interested in those themes might gather. Go there, or organize your own gathering.*

2. *Join a group or network with shared interests, locally or online.*

3. *Find out what local events and festivals are going on in your area and book a ticket.*

4. *Set yourself a physical challenge, either with someone you know or as part of an event already going on, or join a sports team or club.*

5. *Book a spot on a retreat (there is an alchemy in the heady mix of food, fire and open-hearted people) – perhaps a retreat for creativity, yoga, mindfulness, spirituality, ideas, business – just go with what calls to you even if you don't know too much about it, yet.*

6. *Sign up for a workshop or take an online class.*

7. *Go on an adventure.*

8. *Share what inspires you on social media, being creative and putting it out there using whatever medium lights you up.*

9. *Read and comment on blogs and/or start your own.*

10. *Chat to people with similar interests in online forums.*

11. *Arrange to meet someone for coffee with the specific purpose of sharing your dreams.*

12. *Join my secret club,* The Society of Freedom Seekers *(see www.bethkempton.com), to meet other seekers like you, and get support for your journey.*

Then come back and write about it in your journal. You can use this entry to inspire yourself anytime you feel alone or unmotivated. I'd love to know how you get on. Please share what you're up to on social media using #freedomseeker.

⌒∾

Chapter 14

NAVIGATING THE SKIES: CALLING ON THE UNIVERSE FOR GUIDANCE

The question of exactly how birds navigate the skies has been the subject of scientific debate for many years. What we do know is that most birds use a combination of three tools to understand where they are and how to get where they want to go: landmarks, the sun and stars, and the Earth's magnetic field.

Natural landmarks such as mountains and rivers, and man-made landmarks such as tall buildings, can be helpful pointers for birds, but only if they have flown a particular route before. So this first navigational tool is all about **knowledge and experience.**

The sun and the stars are reliable indicators of position and orientation, particularly when the weather is clear. This second tool is therefore all about **information and guidance.**

Then last but not least, birds are thought to use the Earth's magnetic field to navigate. We aren't exactly sure how they do this, although scientists believe birds have a sense called magnetoreception – a kind of inner compass, which allows them to detect the magnetic field and perceive location, altitude and direction. So this third tool is all about using their **sixth sense.**

And so it is with humans, as we try to understand where we are and how to navigate to where we want to go.

First we have to look to our **knowledge and experience** – what we have learned from the road we have taken so far, our background, our education, the books we have read, the conversations we have had, the things said by the people who inspire us, the jobs we have done, the places we have been, all of it.

Then we need to fill in the gaps with **information and guidance.** This is about research, asking questions, talking to people who have done it before, finding role models and mentors, taking classes, gathering information and being prepared to ask for help.

And then there's the third and final tool of navigating life. It's our **sixth sense** – intuition. It's that inner knowing, the answers we already have inside if we just ask and then listen.

If you ignore the first tool you risk repeating past mistakes. If you don't employ the second, you dive blindly into the unknown. But ignoring the third tool is the most dangerous of all, because it is the voice of your free self calling.

∽ Miracles from the edge ∽

By the time that Darin McBratney decided that he no longer wanted to live with the debilitating mystery illness that had taken over his body, he had spent over $400,000 on medical bills, his business was on its knees and his marriage had fallen apart. Darin was not alone, as 22 people in his town had presented similar symptoms and two of them had died. With all hope gone, he decided to take his vintage Porsche up the coast of California and drive off a cliff.

But as he approached Big Sur, he remembered that an old friend lived nearby and felt drawn to call on him. Before he knew it Darin had pulled off the road and found himself at his friend's front door. Having heard Darin's story of suffering, his friend said, 'I think I know a kinesiologist who might be able to help.'

It wasn't any ordinary consultation. The medicine woman took out a collection of old battered suitcases, each filled with hundreds of tiny vials, which appeared empty but were each labelled with the name of a disease.

After doing some energy work with Darin, she proceeded to hover her hands over the suitcases, until she was drawn to a particular group of vials, and then one in particular. 'You have ciguatera,' she told him.

Further tests confirmed the diagnosis, which is also known as 'Red Tide Disease' – so called after the 'red tide' phenomenon of harmful algae blooms that produce toxins in high quantities in the sea. It was likely that Darin was poisoned when he was out surfing. Now desperate for a cure, Darin was crushed to be told 'There is no effective treatment or antidote.' Back to the blackness.

The medicine woman had used something of a miraculous method to get the diagnosis, so Darin printed out a list of every known healing ingredient and asked her to do the same energy work with her hands over the paper, to 'feel' the words. She was unsure but went ahead, spreading his printouts all over the floor and hovering her hands over the words, just as she had with the vials. From time to time she would call out a word, which Darin would scribble down – some were common garden herbs, some were rare plants he had never heard of. Darin gathered all of them, and brought them to the medicine woman, who prepared them for him.

And guess what? The treatment worked. His symptoms disappeared and he made a full recovery. Just like that.

If this miracle really did happen as Darin told it to me, then besides the hopeful implications for anyone else with ciguatera, it's powerful evidence of the importance of allowing ourselves to be guided not only by what we know and get told by others, but by what we feel deep down. It demonstrates just how important it is to listen to what our intuition tells us. If Darin hadn't acted on that pull to visit his old friend, he would never have connected with the medicine woman whose alternative treatment methods saved his life.

In the same way that birds are thought to switch between navigation methods depending on their environment, so we too can manipulate these three navigation tools as and when we need.

*If you consciously choose your
direction of travel and use all these
tools to guide you, then you have
every chance of getting to exactly
where you want to be.*

MORE THAN COINCIDENCE

I used to think I experienced a lot of coincidences. Like the first time I ever went to the arty town of Hebden Bridge in the north of England, and was walking down the road when my phone buzzed with an email from a lady wanting to share her story on my blog. Her name was Alison Bartram and I saw from her email signature that she was the owner of Heart Gallery, in Hebden Bridge. 'Hah, funny!' I thought. 'I'm in her town.'

And then I looked up and realized I was actually standing right outside Heart Gallery. The very same one. Unbelievable.

I went inside to find Alison and introduce myself. She was as surprised as I was, and we thought it only appropriate to go for tea. When we eventually published her story on the blog – a heartbreaking but ultimately uplifting story about how her sister's suicide had led to her quitting her job and following her dream of opening the Heart Gallery – it was a huge inspiration for many of my readers.

Or there was the time I was in the Namib Desert in southern Africa, huddled round a campfire with a group of fellow travellers, when the man next to me started talking about how they had started to do paragliding behind his farm, back in northern Japan. Not long before he left for his travels he saw a foreigner take off and crash back into the hillside. It turns out that foreigner was my older brother (who escaped the crash with just his pride bruised). Instantly there was a point of connection, and the conversations among the group went on late into the night.

And then there was the time I was walking around San Francisco at 5 a.m., woken early by jet lag, dreaming up the idea for a new online course focused on doing what you love in business. I knew what I wanted to share based on my experience in the corporate world, but having only had my own business for a couple of years, I realized I'd need to partner with someone to bring it to life.

I asked myself who my dream collaborator would be and the name 'Kelly Rae Roberts' sprung to mind. (The same Kelly Rae who had taught that retreat workshop a year previously, see page 70). But I hadn't had much contact with her since and she was flourishing in a major way, with a huge online following and explosive success in the world of art licensing. Kelly Rae was way out of my league. But I thought I might as well ask.

So I went back to my hotel and logged onto email only to find an email from Kelly Rae waiting in my inbox. It went something like this:

> *I know this is out of the blue, but I have a feeling we should work on something together. Perhaps something to do with creative business. I'm not sure what yet. What do you think?*

We went on to create 'The Business Soul Sessions' online course, and the 'Hello Soul Hello Business' membership site together, helping creative entrepreneurs all over the world build soulful businesses that generate profits they can be proud of.

As I write this I am in Portland, Oregon, celebrating Kelly Rae's 10-year business milestone. I am deeply grateful and still somewhat incredulous at the depth and longevity of our connection.

GUIDANCE FROM THE UNIVERSE

The truth is, these kinds of things happen to me all the time. They probably happen to you too. It's just a case of noticing. For sure they are coincidences, but there's more to it than the traditional meaning of two things happening at the same time, as if by pure chance. I think it's more about the 'co-incidence' of your direction of travel and the guidance the Universe is sending to you. It goes something like this.

First, when you emerge from your cage, you choose a direction of travel (see figure 2 below). Imagine this as a straight line. You are moving generally in the 'right' direction (towards feeling more free), but the Universe knows about a 'Good Thing' that could be in your future, if you just altered your trajectory slightly.

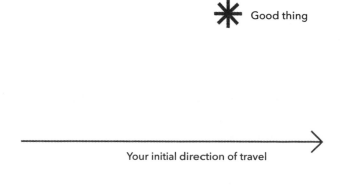

Good thing

Your initial direction of travel

Figure 2: Your direction of travel

In order to let you know about this, the Universe sends you a message about the Good Thing. It tries to capture your attention with a 'co-incidence' at Point A, where its message crosses your path (see figure 3 below). Perhaps it's a note scribbled on the pavement, or the title of an article in a magazine someone leaves on your table at a cafe.

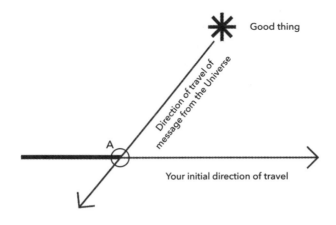

Figure 3: A sign crosses your path

Perhaps you don't notice that sign and keep on travelling in the same direction. So the Universe sends you another message, which crosses your path at Point B, another co-incidence (see figure 4 on page 219). Maybe this time a book falls off the shelf, or an old friend calls you up just as you are thinking about them. Perhaps you think it's a little odd that you keep on seeing the same words, or names, or themes over and over, but you don't do anything about it and just keep travelling along the same path.

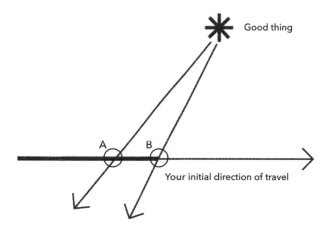

Figure 4: A second sign crosses your path

By now the Universe is getting desperate to capture your attention. You are going so fast in the direction you have chosen that you are completely blinkered and look like you might miss this Good Thing entirely, so the Universe is throwing everything it's got at you. It might be a TV programme, a recurring dream, a wrong number asking for someone of a certain name, a message in graffiti downtown, the announcement of a new workshop popping into your inbox, perhaps even a redundancy notice or a physical illness.

The Universe is prepared to try anything to make sure you don't miss this Good Thing. Point C (see figure 5 on page 220) below shows the co-incidence where you finally take notice, change course (as shown by the emboldened line), and finally head straight for the Good Thing.

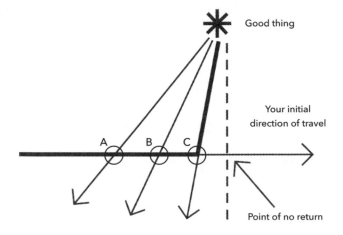

Figure 5: You reach decision point

Each of these co-incidences represents a decision point. If you recognize the signs sent to help you, and then choose to change direction, soon enough you'll discover the Good Thing that has been waiting for you all along.

You can see that the angle through which you have to turn gets bigger the longer it takes you to notice the signs. This means that the longer you leave it to course-correct, the more dramatic the change is likely to be, and the more of a jolt it will feel. So the earlier you start noticing the co-incidences, the gentler (and less scary) the experience of change can be.

There are three ways you can improve your chance of getting to the Good Thing:

1. Slow down.

2. Open your eyes and look.

3. Get quiet and listen.

Of course you can notice a sign but choose to carry on ignoring it. However, if you keep on doing this, eventually you will shoot right on past the Good Thing (past the point of no return in Figure 5 opposite) and it will be gone.

In her brilliant book *Big Magic*, Elizabeth Gilbert shares a genius theory about ideas, and how they go around looking for a human to partner with, trying several times to get one particular human to work with them, but if that person isn't ready or isn't listening, the idea will eventually move on to someone else.

I think it's the same with the Good Things the Universe is trying to tell us about. If we keep ignoring the signs and never even contemplate wavering from the path, we will miss every Good Thing it has to show us – perhaps a job opportunity, or a love prospect, or something else just as juicy. If it wasn't the right time, or we just weren't listening, it will be there for the taking for someone else. That's not to say there aren't other Good Things the Universe can tell us about. There are. But the more Good Things we are drawn to along the way, the better and more fulfilling the journey.

Sometimes I talk about signs and people roll their eyes, but you and I know the truth. One of my friends, Kari Chapin, shared this sweet story recently and it made me laugh out loud.

⁓ Messages from the Universe ⁓

When walking my dogs this afternoon, I noticed a piece of paper fluttering around in the street. I am a saintly type, so I picked it up, thinking it was trash. Since I am in my 40s, I am on the constant lookout for signs from the Universe to, you know, help me make big life decisions. And so when I realized this was a list, I had to read it.

This is what it said:

Glass kiln / Boxes of brushes / Sheets of glass / Blown eggs / Art videos / Fridge, toaster, microwave, dishwasher / Clay / A chicken / Paper! / Skeleton mobile / Glazes / Kiln repair directions / Plugs / Tile cutters / Books

My imagination started running wild. I started thinking... This list is obviously for an art studio, probably a stained glass studio – where you can have some cold rosé (thanks to the fridge), while waiting for your creations (most likely beads) to come out of the glass kiln. The blown eggs threw me a bit, but I'm not one to judge. So I was digging this list, which I was clearly taking as a sign. Until I read it for a second time and noticed 'a chicken'. Why does this person need a chicken? And why did a chicken pop into their mind a little over halfway through making this list? How does this fit? What kind of sign is this after all? What am I supposed to be doing with my life?

This is a fine example of how our brains take something and run with it. And we can choose to let a random list blow in the wind, or we can pick it up, allow it to challenge our imaginations, and take whatever signs from it we like.

Somewhere in there is a story of eggs, chickens, rebirth and the cycle of life. And the fact is, last year Kari took a pottery class, which unexpectedly broke a decade-long streak of depression. Who knew making some lopsided bowls and pencil cups could have made such a big difference? When the class ended, Kari began to feel her depression creep back in, so when she picked up this list, she wondered if it might be a sign to get back in the studio.

You see that's the thing with signs. They may mean something to you, but nothing to someone else. Perhaps not everything you think is a sign is actually a sign, but if it makes you see something differently, think of something new, or remember something you had forgotten, does it even matter? Signs are helpful, and when I am trying to navigate a vast sky, any help is most welcome.

BY THE WAY, THE UNIVERSE ISN'T WAITING FOR YOUR PERMISSION

When I was five years old my mum took my older brother and me to London. We sent our small voices across the Whispering Gallery beneath the soaring dome of St Paul's Cathedral and then met a giant diplodocus skeleton in the Natural History Museum. It was one of those days where you remember all the details, from the ache in your neck from staring up at the blue whale carcass suspended from the ceiling of the biggest room you have ever been in, to the sticky sweetness of the pink Wham bar you ate in one go on a park bench outside, marvelling at the fizzy bits whizzing and popping on your tongue.

For our last treat of the day we slipped into The Science Museum, where they had a Discovery Centre. Everything was hands-on and most of it was awe-inspiring for my young mind. But there was one thing that absolutely captivated me: the plasma globe. It was a giant glass sphere so big I probably could have fitted inside. Tendrils of purple light rippled out from a central glowing orb in seemingly random directions, changing colour when they hit the inside of the sphere wall. They sparked and darted in all directions like lightning trying to escape. It was an otherworldly object that sent my imagination into a spin.

'Put your hand against the glass and see what happens,' said Mum.

Unsure of whether that was really a good idea, in case I released an alien or perhaps got electrocuted, I tentatively reached up and touched it. The glowing tentacles of light shot over to connect my small hand to the centre of the ball. I pressed my palm closer to the glass. Now, instead of the light emanating from the inside, it seemed to be shooting out of me. I was at once terrified and transfixed, and the image was forever scorched onto my brain.

Three decades later, following my creative awakening on that art retreat, I started to notice a huge number of coincidences in my life. I seemed to be making more and more choices based not only on rational analysis, but also a strong sense of intuition and a guidance I couldn't put my finger on. As a logical thinker who had been schooled in mathematical disciplines, I was trying to understand the science behind the concept of a benevolent 'Universe'. I could see the evidence with my own eyes, but had no clue as to the methodology. In fact, I never found the answer in science itself, but it was science that helped me understand, when the image of that plasma globe resurfaced with new meaning.

Now I see it like this. The plasma globe is like the Earth, pulsating with the energy of the Universe, constantly reaching in all directions to offer support wherever it is needed. It's not waiting for your permission. It's working all the time. When you stand still, rooted to the surface, and get quiet and seek guidance, it's like the five-year-old me placing my small hand on the surface of that plasma globe. The crackling bolts of energy are pulled in your direction.

If you only touch the surface lightly – letting yourself be distracted or not really listening – then the effect is only minimal. But if you go all in, slow down and pay attention long enough to really root yourself to the earth and believe that this guidance is available – the equivalent of placing an entire hand firmly against the surface of the plasma ball – then the impact can be astonishing. Clarity, energy, and a sense of immense personal power can hit you like a lightning bolt, as if the energy is surging from within.

But don't forget that you have to play your part. The 'co-incidence' theory only works when you are in motion. There's no point sitting around on your sofa waiting for signs to drop into your lap. You have to be out there, actively looking.

It is when we both pay attention and take action that magic happens.

This is what I think of when I think of 'asking the Universe' for guidance, messages, signs and support. When birds are flying high, they literally 'go with the flow' by taking advantage of air currents to carry them. By working with the Universe, taking notice of signs and following where your navigational tools – knowledge and experience, information and guidance and your sixth sense – are pointing, you too can be carried forward.

TURN ON THE LIGHTS

A short time ago I moved back to my hometown to be near my family for more support while the girls are young. I was anxious about it, because returning there felt like a backward step. But when I looked for signs that it was the right thing to do I found them, and it made the move a whole lot easier.

A week or so before we left Brighton I went for a tarot reading at Two Feathers in North Laine, from a guy named Lee with piercing blue eyes and a tarot deck so well used you could hardly see the pictures. I wanted a sign, any kind of sign, that I was doing the right thing.

From the very first minute Lee was so insightful it made my spine tingle. As soon as I sat down he said 'I sense movement. Are you just about to move house?'

Fluke, perhaps, but then he went on to describe our new house with an uncanny degree of accuracy. He said it was the perfect place for our family to be right now, and there was a protective energy around the house that would mean we would be very happy there. He went on to give insights into private conversations he can't have known anything about.

And then there was the frog.

In the weeks leading up to the reading, Sienna kept saying the word 'frog' over and over. She would just come up to me staring, and keep saying 'frog', completely out of context of what we were talking about or doing at the time. Given she was still in the earliest days of talking, I thought she might just be practising the taste of a new word on her tongue, but it was weird how she said it so often, more so than any other word and she said it only to me.

Towards the end of the reading, Lee said, 'By the way, the whole time you have been sitting here, there's been a frog hovering over your head.' What? Apparently it is a symbol of transition and growth, or rebirth, opportunity and luck. That's what I call a sign. It made me wonder whether Sienna had seen it too, and had been trying to tell me all was going to be OK.

By coincidence (or perhaps not), the Japanese word for 'frog' is *kaeru*, which is also the word for the verb 'to return home'. Funnily enough, once we had moved back to my hometown, there were no more 'frog' outbursts from Sienna.

All the signs are there, we just have to turn on the light to see them, listen carefully, and then trust.

Entry 23: Really listen

Really notice what's going on around you. Take a walk without your headphones on. Leave your phone behind. Look up and all around. Look for anything that feels like a sign, related to the direction you are trying to travel in.

Take photographs. Make notes. Scribble thoughts and observations in your notebook, collect quotes, stickers, labels, ticket stubs, postcards, flyers, anything that feels like it is telling you something. In the beginning you might not know what you are looking for or what it is telling you, but you'll feel yourself drawn to certain things above others. Messages will catch your eye when you're least expecting it.

Post evidence of your signs in your journal. Document what you find. Share your discoveries on social media using #freedomseeker so we can wonder at them too. Start talking about it. See what happens.

LISTEN TO YOUR BODY

Your body is a powerful communicator of your intuition. Sometimes it speaks in pleasure, sometimes in pain. Sometimes it is just a dull ache, suggesting things aren't quite right.

When you are trying to navigate to somewhere new, pay attention, because your body may just hold the clues you need to find your way.

~ Feeling grounded ~

As she counted down the weeks to finishing a work project in Seattle, AnneLiese Nachman booked a flight to Arizona, departing as soon as her contract had ended. She had been pining for the outdoors from inside her cubicle, and decided to give herself a chance to breathe in fresh air for a couple weeks instead of jumping right into her next job hunt. The trip would be her first experience climbing outdoors instead of in rock gyms, and when the time came, she loved every minute of it.

Returning to Seattle, AnneLiese started applying for jobs, but soon became depressed. She went climbing in the gym to ease the stress, and felt right at home, but back at her desk the anguish returned. The more she thought about committing any longer to a normal life in the city, the more her body ached.

AnneLiese developed a painful knot in her lower back, so she joined a yoga class to see if it would ease the discomfort. By coincidence (or not), the class had a theme of groundedness, exactly what AnneLiese really needed in her life at that point.

The instructor suggested that the class find a way to incorporate things that make them feel grounded into their weekly routines. She smiled at the thought of climbing outside weekly, and felt a release of the tension she had been holding in her lower back – the location of the root chakra and source of that sense of groundedness.

Now AnneLiese works as a filmmaker, specializing in short films about climbing and adventure. Since starting to listen to her body, she has navigated her way to a new lifestyle via the stunning scenery of Yosemite National Park, Red Rock Canyon and Moab in Utah. She has never been happier, or felt more free.

Entry 24: Decision making with the help of the Universe

When you find yourself having to make a decision about your direction of travel, try tuning in to your intuition to help you decide. If you find that hard, or don't know how to do it, try this:

1. *Look at the choices in front of you. Let's pretend they are YES and NO. Take the first choice and try it on for size. Imagine you have chosen YES.*

Now notice how you feel in your body. Check in on your energy levels. How is your breathing? Do you have any feelings of heaviness or lightness? Do you have sweaty palms? Do you feel happy about the decision, or terrified? If you feel terrified, is it excited-terrified or oh-no-what-have-I-done-terrified? Do you feel tension or expansion? Is your heart racing or fluttering? In your journal, write down how you are feeling.

2. *Now try on the second choice for size. Imagine you have chosen NO. Run through the checklist again. What is your body telling you? Again, write down how you are feeling.*

3. *Now decide. What will you choose?*

～

Chapter 15

TURBULENCE: COPING WHEN LIFE THROWS YOU A CURVEBALL

If I've learned anything from these cycles of incarceration and escape, it's that life never unfolds as we expect. Sometimes we are showered with unexpected blessings and sometimes bad things happen. I call this turbulence.

Turbulence can hit at any time. When life throws you a curveball, it can feel like being punched in the stomach and sent careering into a spin. Everything you thought you knew is thrown into question, and it's as if you are being sucked into a vortex. Often it happens so fast you don't even realize what's going on until you are deep in it. You go into survival mode. Sometimes it feels like you might not make it through. You get extreme clarity regarding your priorities, and nothing else matters for a while.

Anyone who has experienced turbulence on a plane knows how uncomfortable it can be. It's actually rare for the shaking, lurching and apparent lack of control to cause real injury, but it can be terrifying. If a pilot knows it's coming he or she will warn the passengers, but the most common form – Clean Air Turbulence – is also the most disturbing because it cannot be predicted. It is invisible to the eye and undetectable by radar.

In our lives, the equivalent of Clean Air Turbulence is that shocking piece of news that comes out of the blue. The telephone call saying a friend has been in an accident, your child is ill, or your landlord hasn't paid his mortgage and you're being evicted. It's your own health scare, or the moment you find out your spouse is having an affair, or that your business partner has screwed you over.

And sometimes, your worst nightmare actually happens.

∼ Drifting fragments ∼

'I felt like a vase that had been dropped on the floor and smashed into a million pieces,' my childhood friend Holly Deacon recalls, trying to describe her emotions in the aftermath of her younger sister Bryony's suicide. 'It was as if I shattered on impact, and then watched the pieces float away in slow motion. Over the next two weeks I could see myself reaching for one fragment at a time, but it was an effort to stretch and often the pieces would drift just beyond reach.'

In those two weeks of bone-shaking turbulence, while she waited for the autopsy and funeral, Holly functioned on autopilot. Writing invitations for her son's upcoming 10th birthday party took her eight hours. Friends rallied round, but looking back, she has no idea what anyone said. Her nights were haunted and her days were filled with black, confused thoughts. It was all she could do to feed her children and put one foot in front of the other. Life would never be the same again.

Shortly after Bryony's death, Holly was scheduled to join a small gathering of friends up north. Initially she was going to cancel, but then decided it might do her some good to get away for a couple of days. Those friends huddled round her, wrapping her in a blanket of love and helping her grasp back some of the drifting fragments.

Driving home in the dark she felt something shift. Mumford & Sons' 'I Will Wait' came on the radio, and she released a torrent of tears.

'That car journey home was my first clear memory since the day it happened,' she recalls. As Holly is telling me this, she suddenly stops in amazement. The exact same song has just come on over the cafe speakers, as if Bryony herself is sending us a message.

Now we are both crying.

I ask Holly if time really does heal. 'It helps,' she says. 'The sadness will always be there, but I know the shape of it now. I can recognize it, acknowledge it, and still carry on with my day.'

Now the shattered vase has been put back together, with love and hope and courage. Some of the cracks are still visible, and there's a chip here and there, but they add character and beauty, and in some ways the vessel is even stronger than before.

In Holly's case, once the turbulence had abated, she found herself trapped in a cage of anxiety and grief, so she used the Freedom Key of Creativity + Innovation to find a way to express what she was going through, and escape. She used art to help the healing process, rebuilding the vase piece by piece and reclaiming that inner space in the process.

BEAUTY IN THE BROKENNESS

When we see someone in pain after a traumatic experience, our tendency is often to try to fix them, but usually that's neither what they need, nor what we should offer. They can't be put back together as before because they are forever changed. We can only offer support for their own reconstruction process, knowing that it is a delicate and often long road.

Remember, freedom is the willingness and ability to choose your own path and experience your life as your true self. To allow others to be free is to allow them to experience their life as their true selves too.

Turbulence is part of the experience of life. It's one of the ways we grow. Sometimes you will learn a lesson that takes you closer to your true self. Sometimes it's about finding a way to deal with the pain.

In Japan there is a traditional craftsmanship called *kintsugi*, which is the art of repairing broken pottery using lacquer dusted with gold. This philosophy embraces the shattering as part of the rich history of the object. And so it can be with us. We don't have to hide the cracks and the broken bits. They are part of who we are becoming.

It's hard to recognize this when you are being battered by the chaos, but know that turbulence always passes, and the calm will eventually return.

When turbulence hits

Turbulence tends to come from negative things, but positive things can shake you up too. The unexpected promotion that means relocating, the sudden success of a creative venture that requires you to start speaking in public, an unplanned pregnancy. Whatever it is that takes you by surprise, it can come out of nowhere and shake everything up.

The only thing you know for sure is that turbulence will hit at some point. You can't prevent it, but you can prepare yourself.

From my own experience, and the stories of hundreds of people in my community, I have identified three actions to help deal with turbulence. They have worked for me in the past, and Holly recognized them to be exactly how she coped in the aftermath of Bryony's death. Knowing about these steps in advance can help you ride out the turbulence when it inevitably strikes. The three actions are:

1. Breathe
2. Wing tuck
3. Huddle

Step 1: Breathe

Take a moment to stop and breathe. Just concentrate on your breath. In, out. In, out. Sit down if you need to. Keep breathing. As deeply as you can, and let the oxygen flow to your brain.

Then establish the facts. If at all possible, eliminate conjecture and concentrate on what you know to be true right now. This will help you take any necessary action with minimal panic.

Then, however that action makes you feel, allow yourself to feel it and keep breathing.

Step 2: Wing tuck

Birds experience the same turbulence as planes, but handle it differently. A study by scientists at Oxford University, published by The Royal Society in 2014, tracked a steppe eagle's flight through more than 2,500 instances of turbulence and discovered that it made a very smart move every time. In order to avoid being buffeted by the wind, the eagle folded its wings beneath its body, for around 0.35 seconds, so it briefly plummeted to avoid the worst of it. This is known as a 'wing tuck'. According to Professor Graham Taylor, the scientist leading the research, 'Rather like the suspension on a car, birds use this technique to dampen the potentially damaging jolting caused by turbulence.'

If we translate this to ourselves when experiencing life turbulence, it makes perfect sense. When things are really tough, tucking in our wings, scaling back commitments and retreating into what is most important, even for a very short time, can help cushion the blow.

It's OK to cancel that meeting, or say no to that work request. It's OK not to bake cakes for the school fundraiser this year. It's OK to ask for a deadline extension, or take a week off. Of course it is important to communicate these 'wing tucks' to anyone affected, but it's vital that you don't just soldier on because people need you.

In times of turbulence, YOU need you. Go for a long walk, try to eat well, take a hot bath. Journal. Light a candle. Sleep if you can. Do whatever feels nurturing to you. Be kind and gentle to yourself.

Step 3: Huddle

If you were ever going to call on your flock for support, now is the time. Not only might they ease the pressure of some of your commitments, but they can encourage you through the turbulence when you cannot see ahead. Know that people may not know what to say, but worrying about that is not your responsibility right now.

When friends rally round give them practical things to do: bring dinner, take your children to school, walk the dog, clean your house. You can ask someone to be a buffer between you and the rest of the world, or just ask for a hug and hold them close.

If someone you know is experiencing turbulence, you can encourage them to breathe, wing tuck and huddle. Don't worry about not knowing what to say, or not knowing how to fix it. It's not your job to fix it. It's being there that matters the most. Just do what you can. And love them more than ever.

Entry 25: Caught in it

Think of a time you have been caught in turbulence, and think about how you dealt with it. Write an entry in your journal detailing what happened and how you felt and coped.

Now run through the breathe, wing tuck and huddle steps above and see what could have helped you at the time. Make some notes to remind you next time.

If you are caught in turbulence right now, just breathe, wing tuck and huddle.

STIRRING IT UP

Turbulence is the messy, uncomfortable part that happens when your context rapidly changes; usually due to things that life throws at you.

However, sometimes we actually create that turbulence by whipping up the air with a flurry of changes ourselves, too much, too soon. Not long ago, this happened to us. After making a series of major life changes in rapid succession, my husband and I finally felt we were starting to soar. But just as we settled into that we flew headlong into turbulence and our whole world went into flux.

My husband woke in the middle of the night with chest pains and shortness of breath. Before I knew it, there were three paramedics in our bedroom, examining him for evidence of a potential heart attack. Mr K is 39, fit and strong, and the love of my life. It was devastating.

I was on autopilot packing for the hospital, getting the car seat ready for our baby to join us in the ambulance, and making sure I had a phone charger and change. My older brother, Jon, had left home as soon as I called, to come and watch over our sleeping daughter while we went to the hospital, but it would be half an hour before he arrived.

I called on a neighbour to ask her to babysit until Jon arrived. Hazel opened the door in her pyjamas, with big hair, red eyes, and an understandable look of concern. At that moment I crumbled, and could hardly get the words out past my tears. My beautiful husband, who has the biggest heart I know, might have just had a coronary.

The next few hours were a blur, with machines and tests and questions and more tests. As I sat waiting with my baby girl in my arms, my head was flooded with 'what ifs' and 'please nots'.

Thankfully Mr K's heart tests all came back clear, and he made a full recovery. Later we were told that it was probably 'just' a panic attack, possibly brought on by the tumultuous change in our lives recently – the birth of a new baby with the ensuing sleepless nights, a toddler starting to tantrum, a house move to a new city where we hardly knew anyone, a busy time with our business and very little time to relax.

We knew that we had been juggling a lot, but had felt like we were just about managing. We were enjoying exploring the new shape of our little family, and the business was flourishing. We hadn't noticed how stressed we actually were in the midst of so much change.

In the end Mr K was fine, and hasn't had any more panic attacks. I have no doubt this is due to cutting back on commitments and taking better care of ourselves.

When you realize you want to take a different path, and you can see the way ahead, it's tempting to rush things. But take it easy, one step at a time, so you don't trigger that turbulence yourself. Don't make too many changes at once. And make sure you pay extra attention to your wellbeing and that of those you share your life with, each step of the way.

CAUGHT IN TURBULENCE OR TRAPPED IN THE CAGE?

Being caught in turbulence is hard, and being trapped in a cage is hard. In some ways they can feel similar, but actually they are worlds apart.

Turbulence is short-lived. It's the rapid changing of your context, and the confusion and disorientation that comes with a sideswipe from life. Being trapped in a cage is more protracted. It is the inertia that sets in when you get stuck in a rut. When you're trapped in the cage you're grasping at the bars. When you're caught in turbulence, you're gasping for air. Both are exhausting and stressful and limiting. One can lead to the other, and both hamper your flight. I want to share my friend Lisa's heartbreaking but inspiring story to demonstrate the difference.

~ Against the odds ~

When Lisa Moncrieff found out she was expecting a baby girl, she was thrilled. She imagined all the things they would do together, the places they would go and experiences they would share. However, Rosie was born with a rare disease, nemaline rod myopathy, a rare form of muscular dystrophy, and two-thirds of babies born with this condition don't live beyond two years old.

The first couple of months of Rosie's life were a period of dark turbulence for Lisa and her husband, Iain, as they saw their lives turned upside down. They closed ranks, dropped everything that wasn't important, and called on family and close friends for support. Breathe. Wing tuck. Huddle.

As time went on, they found themselves settling into a very difficult context, with Lisa returning to work and Iain quitting his career to become Rosie's full-time carer. They became trapped in a cage of worry, monotony, frustration and guilt.

Just before her first birthday, Rosie caught a cold, and with an immune system that couldn't cope, went into respiratory arrest and medically died in her father's arms. Miraculously the hospital staff got there in time and resuscitated her, just as Lisa arrived on the ward.

Following Rosie's recovery, Lisa and Iain somehow managed to settle into a kind of normality at home, even if their house was filled with all manner of machinery, gadgets and drugs to keep Rosie alive. Iain became Rosie's full-time carer again while Lisa went back to work. But as time went on, Lisa found she was distancing herself from friends who had had babies at a similar time, because it was too painful. Losing this support network only added to the pressure. Lisa and Iain's relationship understandably suffered too.

It felt like the cage was closing in around them, until Christmas Day, a few months before Rosie's second birthday. The three of them were supposed to be spending Christmas with family, but Rosie's young cousin had a cold, so the trip was cancelled at the last minute. Lisa and Iain woke up on Christmas Day alone with their little girl, with no plans and no need to be anywhere.

Lisa felt herself do one long exhale. They hadn't really expected to get to this point and still have Rosie with them, but she was as healthy as she had ever been, and full of personality. They felt happy as a family, and proud of themselves as they reflected on everything they had endured in the past year.

Lisa's exhale was followed by a slow inhale of the peace and quiet. They spent the day having fun together, then began to think about what they wanted to do in the coming year. Lisa felt something shift.

Without realizing it, that Christmas Day Lisa and Iain activated their Freedom Keys of Playfulness + Curiosity, and Connection + Communication, to escape the cage they had both been trapped in. Ever since they have taken care to really talk to each other, be aware of how the other is feeling, and support each other in a whole new way. They have planned more fun days out with Rosie, and recently celebrated the huge milestone of her second birthday.

They are still living in the same context, but are now virtually free of the cage bars. Rather than feeling guilt, frustration and loneliness, Lisa now feels gratitude for all her brave daughter has taught her, a deeper connection than ever to her wonderful husband, and a togetherness, that they are experiencing this as a family.

In Lisa's case, she suffered turbulence when she first found out how sick her young daughter was. It threw her life, and her husband's life, into complete chaos. They were wholly unprepared for the life-altering implications of their daughter's illness.

Eventually this bombshell settled into being the new context in which Lisa's life was playing out. There have been times when she has felt trapped, but once her context became more familiar, and she recognized her cage, she used her Freedom Keys to escape and is now incredibly grateful for the gift of her precious daughter, just as she is.

The only sure-fire way to avoid turbulence is not to fly in the first place, but that is no way to live.

Brace yourself, but don't fly in fear. Know that preparation is half the battle, and that as a Freedom Seeker, the work you have done already makes you stronger and more resilient than ever. You have everything you need to ride out the storm —whatever life throws your way. Just remember to breathe, wing tuck and huddle.

YOU WILL GET THROUGH IT

If you are caught up in turbulence right now, I want you to hear this.

You are doing great. You will be OK in the end.

It may feel like the sky is caving in, and you are tumbling in freefall not knowing which way is up.

You may want to scream out loud, or shrink into silence.

You may be desperate for answers, or have no idea of the questions.

It's OK. You will be OK.

Just breathe, wing tuck and huddle.

Chapter 16

STAYING AIRBORNE: FUELLING YOUR JOURNEY

As I pushed aside guilt, worry and the demands on my time, I made space for peace, rest, new inspiration, new ideas, new recognition of the real me. I rediscovered my love of writing, my love of nature and the outdoors, the sheer joy in laughter. And as I let go of my preconceptions of the kind of parent, wife and friend I should be, I found a way to become the parent, wife and friend I already was. When I looked inside I discovered my own brave heart and I felt strong again.

It was only after my bedroom floor moment, when I started looking at every area of my life with new eyes, that I suspected just how much money we were haemorrhaging each month. I went to my favourite cafe, ordered a cappuccino and sat at the breakfast bar with my bank and credit card statements. I made notes of everything we were spending, shocked at what was scribbling itself across the page. Left to build up over a year, my daily coffee habit would have flown me round the world twice. Our rent would cover an average salary. Let's not mention what we spent on food – mostly ready meals from expensive supermarkets to save time. I totalled it up and felt physically sick. The irony was we hardly went out socializing. We didn't have a car. We didn't really buy much 'stuff'. We were just bleeding money in order to live in this big house, to keep the wheels turning, continually pushing to get who-knows-where... Enough!

I made a decision there and then to stop wasting my precious resources – time, money, energy. Instead of throwing money at problems to make them go away, Mr K and I made wholesale changes that would make us feel more free. Like downsizing and moving city to halve our monthly outgoings. Like making home feel more homely, so we'd spend less money eating out. Like sorting my clothes so I knew what I actually had, instead of just buying more.

Mr K shared his ideas about feeling free, and we discussed how we could raise our children to feel free too. We thought about the environment we were providing, the energy and the atmosphere in the house, about how we could make that our sanctuary. We invited our free selves to sit at the kitchen table and contribute to family meetings. 'What if anything was possible? What would we do then? What if we could start over? What would we do differently? What if all that mattered was being happy? What would we do next?'

We took a fresh look at our business, Do What You Love, which I had set up six years previously, and Mr K had joined just after we got married. As an online business, in theory it gives us complete freedom to work when we want, from where we want. But we had become slaves to the machine that we had built. We had developed several partnerships and produced a raft of powerful courses that had supported thousands of people worldwide to live happier, more creative and inspired lives. But in doing so, we had raced to keep up with the success, growing our team to keep up with demand, without stopping to ask whether it was the direction we wanted to take.

I didn't want to let anyone down. I wanted to be seen as capable, on top of things. And so I kept saying 'Yes' when I should have sometimes said 'No', or 'Not right now'. I kept adding to my list, instead of throwing it away and following my heart. I kept doing the thing I was good at, because it was expected, and because I had said I would do it, rather than doing the thing I needed to do, which was rest, and the things I wanted to do, which were many, and mostly nothing to do with being at my desk.

At the time I most needed to concentrate on my babies and my own wellbeing, I had overcommitted and overextended myself. Business can be a gateway to freedom, but only if you set it up in a way that allows you to feel delight in the everyday. If your daily reality and routine makes you feel trapped, it makes no difference whether the big picture promises freedom. You won't feel it.

When I began Do What You Love, I was the guide. I shared my thoughts and truths about the world through the courses I created and led. In time the success of those courses brought others to my door – strong, inspiring women with a gift and passion for teaching. More by accident than by design, I became the producer, and it has been a great honour to support their work by delivering the infrastructure that has allowed them to share their wisdom so widely. Working with those women has been one of my most precious and valuable professional experiences, and I am grateful for it. But when I made the decision to escape the cage, and emerged from the fog, I realized I needed something for myself too. That didn't mean I had to sacrifice the business that I had built, but rather I could reshape it to allow my own projects to flourish alongside those already in place.

In the end it was a simple equation. The more time I spent with Sienna and Maia, the closer we became. The more time I spent with Mr K, the more I remembered why I married him. The more time I spent alone, the more I reconnected with my free self and discovered what made me feel alive. And the more I did all this, the more I showed up in every other area of my life.

We think we don't have enough time, but actually we have plenty. It's just a case of how we choose to spend it. That doesn't mean I don't have busy days, it doesn't mean I don't have a to-do list, it doesn't mean I don't sometimes collapse into bed wondering where the day went. But more often nowadays it means I spend it in ways that make me feel free, in moments that matter, with people I love, doing things that I love. That makes me happier, and that makes those around me happier.

Besides getting more conscious about how we spent our time, money and energy, we became actively grateful. For the precious moments of childhood, parenthood and marriage. For chocolate, bubble baths and cosy blankets. For evenings by the woodburner and nights in the moonlight. For wandering in nature and standing barefoot on the grass. For conversation and quiet time. For crazy dancing and laughing until it hurt. For old friends and new friends. For cuddles, shared secrets and bedtime stories. For Mr K and I finally finding a way to be masters of our destiny. For each other and the shared journey.

Just as becoming disconnected from my free self was not a single dramatic moment, neither was our reconciliation. We slowly and gently felt our way back to each other. We sought out small moments of joy and delight, turned towards our experiences and felt our way through them. And in time this added up to a reunion, and a sense of freedom once again.

PLAY THE LONG GAME

The ideal lifestyle for a Freedom Seeker is one that allows you to feel free every single day.

I have come to understand that in order to live like this, you need to take two approaches simultaneously:

1. Activate your Freedom Keys to feel free in the moment as often as possible

2. Use your Freedom Keys as a guide to make choices which will set up a lifestyle that invites freedom in for the long term

By now you know how to activate your Freedom Keys and soak in the precious moments of those experiences.

Now it's time to talk about playing the long game – about understanding what you are prepared to sacrifice or endure temporarily in order to create a new kind of lifestyle for yourself, in the long run.

Let's take a look at the example of a Freedom Seeker who had a dream, like so many of us do, of opening his own cafe. Meet my friend Spencer Bowman.

~ Freedom in the long run ~

Spencer is a Freedom Seeker at heart, and gave up his corporate job and a healthy salary to take on the challenge of owning his own coffee shop. Three years on Mettricks now has four locations across Hampshire in the UK, and is rapidly making a name for itself as a provider of delicious coffee, great food and a home-from-home welcome. It's also my second office.

But to stop there would be to gloss over what has oftentimes been a very tough road.

In the past three years Spencer has seen it all – being gazumped for new units, late-running construction work in front of his premises, criminal damage to his property, spiralling staff costs and more. The business nearly went under in the early days. He stopped buying clothes and going on holidays, and didn't pay himself a salary until recently. In the end he split up with his girlfriend under the stress of it all.

In many ways Spencer had fled one cage only to trap himself in another, with the pressure of salaries to pay, demands on his time and the reality of being attached to a particular physical location.

Not long ago, after the eighth break-in in less than a year, Spencer found himself alone in his flagship cafe after hours, head in hands, in floods of tears, his mind searching for an exit route. Should he just jack it all in and sell up?

But then he lifted his head to the family pictures hanging on the cafe wall, and thought back to his childhood and his grandparents' home. They had five children, lots of grandchildren and dozens of great-grandchildren, so the place was always overrun with people, laughter and love. He remembered that had been his inspiration when he started Mettricks – a place where people of all ages could feel at home. People need that in their community, and he realized how happy it made him to see it coming to life, despite the challenges.

Spencer also reminded himself of the many reasons he loves this new path he has chosen: his fantastic staff, the connections, the stories, the opportunities for creativity and using his initiative, the chance to play a role in shaping his city, and injecting life into the community.

He tried on what it would feel like to walk away, and then he tried on what it would feel like to stay. There was no contest. He chose to stay. But it helped to remind himself that he always has a choice.

This reaffirmed his commitment to playing the long game. Spencer has found ways to feel free within his day-to-day, even alongside challenging issues, and he continues to build his business to also set him up for freedom in the long run.

The fact is, many Freedom Seekers dream big, and bringing big dreams to life takes time. The flight path towards big dreams is rarely easy and never straight. I have discovered this myself. I can't imagine going back to a corporate job, but that isn't to say things aren't challenging on the path that I have chosen. The difference is knowing you have a choice, and making that choice to feel free each time.

Remember, the challenges are the context. Whether you allow yourself to get trapped again depends on how you respond to that context.

Some challenges and sacrifices are par for the course, but if the quest for feeling free in the long term is too painful day-to-day, perhaps there's another path you could try. Pain is a clue for navigating in flight. It warns us off things, away from certain people and situations, and towards others. It reminds us of things we have already learned. In some ways we actually need it to navigate the vast sky of life.

Take time to check in with your Freedom Keys again, and see if you can find a way to feel more free today, while setting yourself up to feel more free in the future too.

TRAPPED BY SUCCESS

Sometimes, after spending years striving for something, we finally get it and then realize it isn't actually making us happy. This is devastating, confusing and disorienting. Sometimes it happens because we have been measuring ourselves against someone else's version of success. Or we have set a goal and pursued it doggedly, without checking in along the way, to see if it is still what we actually want. And sometimes the pursuit of success simply takes so long that our entire context has changed by the time we finally 'get there'.

~ Through the cage bars ~

At school Robert John Gorham wasn't 'the sporty one', 'the academic one' or 'the arty one'. He excelled in throwing parties. This led him to a career in music, and success as a hugely popular DJ on BBC Radio 1, known as Rob da Bank. When his career was at its peak, he and his wife Josie, along with two co-founders, created 'Bestival', a music festival that would go on to become one of the biggest parties of them all, winning many awards including 'Best Major Festival in the UK'.

Attracting tens of thousands of people every year, it has spawned numerous spin-off events and is run by a dedicated team of people who Rob considers to be family. Yet lately, once each event is over and he goes back to the day-to-day reality of dealing with suppliers, taking overall responsibility for a huge budget but slim profit margin and making decisions that have nothing to do with music, he has been sensing that something doesn't feel quite right. At the age of 43, at the peak of his fame and career, Rob da Bank is feeling slightly trapped.

'Bestival is amazing in so many ways – the people, the experience, the energy, the celebration. But the truth is, a lot of the time I actually wish that I had a 9–5 job, on a regular wage, letting someone else be responsible,' he tells me. I am taken aback. First impressions suggest that Rob is a non-conformer through and through, and yet it appears he is deadly serious.

The trouble is when Rob and his co-founders sketched out the idea for Bestival over a decade ago they never imagined it would be such an explosive success. How ironic that the ambitious dream, which started out as a way to be independent and free, has become so successful that it has started to strip that personal freedom away.

This modest man with a gentle face and cheeky smile has just shown me his latest creation – the world's biggest bouncy castle – commissioned for Common People, a spin-off event in my hometown of Southampton. There is an excitement in his voice as he explains where the idea came from, and he clearly cannot wait to have his first bounce. Rob is a fan of world records. Bestival also holds the record for the largest disco ball, and the most people in fancy dress in one place. It's this innate sense of fun that has made

Bestival a favourite in the UK's music calendar. But there's not so much fun in the day-to-day work Rob is doing, and that has set an alarm bell ringing.

Rob cares deeply about Bestival. He believes in it, and has an ambitious vision for its growth. But Rob also writes film scores, owns a record label and wants to spend more time with his young family. He also just wants to make more music for himself, but the festival dominates, consuming 90 per cent of his working week.

In the long term Rob has many options, from giving staff new responsibilities to selling the festival to a buyer with a vision as ambitious as his. But right now, trapped in the cage, it's often hard to see a way out. As Rob da Bank stares through the cage bars, he can see his free self at his decks with his headphones on, smiling as he pumps out great tunes at a special party for his young family and closest friends. That party is called Life, and he wants back in.

If you're a Freedom Seeker trapped by your own success, you are not alone. Imagine you are on the outside looking down at your own cage. Doesn't it seem both crazy and sad that you are stuck, having worked so hard to get exactly where you are?

Take a moment to recognize how far you've come, what you've achieved and how proud you can be.

Many of us take a 'project' approach to our lives: starting new things with excitement, building them up to a peak and then gradually losing interest as things change, and as we change. We flourish and grow in cycles. Numerology tells us those cycles are nine years long. Within that, you might also have a shorter 'project cycle'.

Projects have different stages – ideation, creation, implementation, reward and reflection – and the project cycles vary in length from person to person. Mine's about three years. Yours might be longer, or shorter, before your attention starts to wander and you need a new 'project' – a new phase of life with something new to sink your teeth into, inspire you and help you grow further.

Whatever your project cycle length, knowing where you are in that cycle can help you manage your energy, know when to be on the lookout for new opportunities, and understand why your emotional response to any given project may be changing over time.

If you force yourself to remain in the same 'project' beyond its natural life cycle, or without evolving the project to suit where you are today, you'll find yourself trapped. This doesn't mean you have to quit your job, or split up with your partner or make some other huge life change every time you get to the end of a cycle. But it does mean you need to check in with yourself and innovate your situation – or the project itself – around the time the cycle is coming to a close. And perhaps a new project is actually exactly what you need.

Not long ago my parents moved house and discovered a box of my old scrapbooks in the attic. Each collection of fading sugar paper pages had the hallmark of a reporter at work, carefully documenting everywhere we went and everything I ate every holiday of my childhood. Whenever I was bored, I would ask my parents for a project – I needed something to make or research, or a mystery to solve, and it seems some things never change.

When I most recently felt trapped, my business was flourishing and I was grateful to be working with inspiring and dedicated business partners, but in the drive to achieve our shared ambitions, I had sacrificed my personal dreams. The answer was not to ditch everything that had gone before and start again, but rather, simply, to have my own project as well. With hindsight it is so obvious, but at the time I didn't see it. Now I know it's possible to do both, by making different choices.

Entry 26: Mapping your project cycles

Think back over the main milestones in your life and see if there is a pattern in the length of time between them. If major things have happened to you unexpectedly, like an illness or bereavement, this may disrupt the pattern, but look closely at situations where you have actively made a change.

Make notes in your journal and see if you can identify the approximate length of your key life projects. (You might consider time in any given job or particular role, within a given company, in a relationship or living in a given place, for example.) There is no right or wrong answer. Everyone is different.

If you have spotted a pattern, where are you in the latest cycle? Is something coming to an end? Are you halfway through? Is something just beginning?

Think back to the key moments you have felt trapped before. How do these correspond with the project cycles? Do you have a tendency to feel trapped at a particular point in a cycle? What did you change last time? How did you escape? What does this tell you about where you are now, and what you might do next?

RESOURCE-FULL

What does 'success on your terms' look like? Many of us tend to think in terms of money, but that is just one of several precious resources we have at our disposal, such as time, energy and attention. And these resources are a means to an end, not the end itself.

Just think how we use financial verbs to describe how we use these resources – invest time, spend money, give energy, pay attention. Try thinking of these resources as inputs, not outputs or outcomes. Once you stop seeing them as the destination, and start seeing them as fuel for your journey, you realize that they are actually vehicles of freedom. We need to use them as efficiently and effectively as possible so they serve us well.

How do you prioritize how you spend yours? If you are serious about shaking things up and following a new path, you need to consider how you are spending the resources you have, to ensure they are supporting your Flight Plan.

Know that the sacrifices and investments you make in doing what you love come back in spades. Every minute, every dollar, every ounce of energy and attention, if invested in the right direction, will bring you untold riches of the most important kind.

And remember, you get to choose. Really. You do.

~ Keep your options open ~

Kate Hadley lives off-grid in a forest, in a sweet wooden house her husband Geoff built from two gypsy caravans. They run a rural craft school and outdoor theatre group, hosting woodland banquets, teaching woodworking and offering workshops at music festivals in the summer. Kate and Geoff had their second child, a baby girl, just a few months ago, so they are taking fallow time to be together. There is a living, breathing authenticity to their home and to their lives.

To Kate, success means self-sufficiency and a sense of happiness living in nature. The family lives hand-to-mouth, but has no debt. In contrast, many of Kate's urban friends have huge bills and owe thousands. Kate doesn't judge whether one way is better than the other, but knows that she'd rather pay for her meals in sweat and time, rather than commute to a job she doesn't want so she can buy food from a supermarket.

Although I know Kate's way of living is too extreme for me right now, I was inspired by its simplicity when I visited her. The principle here is about living according to what makes you feel free, and that is a possibility for all of us.

Until not long ago Mr K and I lived in a buzzing city by the sea. It was a fantastic place to be, but it was very expensive. Moving somewhere cheaper took away the pressure to work so hard to pay for everything. And when you put your spending in the context of what else you could be doing with it, you soon get clarity. Within a few months of moving away, the reduction in our monthly outgoings could have bought round-the-world tickets for our entire family. Ultimately, lowering the bills was a simple step towards feeling more free.

What could you simplify in your life that would free you up for the things that really matter?

Build a Flight Fund

I encourage you to consider building a personal Flight Fund, starting right now. This is an emergency buffer for that moment in the future when you can feel the cage bars coming back, and you need to activate your Freedom Keys. Set aside whatever you can afford each month and watch it grow.

It may be that you will need to buy a plane ticket, or quit your job and be able to survive three months without pay. Perhaps you will need to purchase art supplies so you can dive deep into your creativity, or pay a film crew to make a video of you campaigning for something you believe in. You might need seed funding to start a new business. Whatever it is, when you need to escape the cage, your Flight Fund will mean that a lack of money doesn't hold you back. It can help you switch from 'I can't afford to…' to 'I can't afford not to…'

If you create a Flight Fund in advance, then when the time comes to use it, you won't add the pressure of money worries to your situation, and you will be proud of yourself for having built it up. It's just one more way of giving yourself choices.

MAKE THE MOST OF NOW

We often give our attention to things that weigh us down, but by worrying about them we only serve to make them heavier. Focusing on anything that is at odds with your Freedom Keys adversely affects your flight. Don't let it. Choose something else to pay attention to.

Whether or not you love the things you currently spend most of your time doing, paying attention to your Freedom Keys within that context can really help.

For example, if you are stuck in a boring job and one of your Freedom Keys is Creativity + Innovation (see page 69), you could start by making your workspace beautiful, designing signs for company events, or coming up with new ways of doing things.

If one of your Freedom Keys is Connection + Communication (see page 89), you could make it your mission to tease out the secret lives of your colleagues, or get your company to pay for you to take a training course in NLP. There is always a way to subversively bring your Freedom Keys into any situation. The harder it is, or the more unlikely it seems, the more triumphant you feel as you do it, and the more interesting every day becomes.

~ Enjoying the ride ~

After six years in the same job, Lucy Hill took a three-month sabbatical and travelled, took photographs and wrote extensively. While she was away she realized that she loved her job, but craved a more creative life. Instead of making a major change, Lucy discovered that she could feel more free simply by being more creative at work, and in the spare minutes of her day.

Now she listens to inspiring podcasts as she walks, writes blog content on the train, reads books in her lunch break and always carries her camera and journal in her bag. Perhaps the biggest transformation has come from unleashing her creativity in the workplace. Lucy has put herself forward to create advertising campaigns, training courses and booklets, and in doing so has allowed herself to be more creative while delivering to a higher standard for her employer.

At weekends she is studying for a qualification that will expand her horizons, and she has set up a small space in her attic as a studio. Ultimately Lucy wants her own business, but for now she is staying in the same job and building the foundations of her new company on the side. It's a sensible approach, which takes time, but the chances of success are high, and she is enjoying the ride.

As you go about your day, be conscious of what you are giving your attention to. Focus on the things you want to cultivate and nurture. Don't allow yourself to be distracted by things that don't really matter.

Remember, paying attention is essential for feeling free, because it is a crucial part of experiencing your own life.

Entry 27: Freedom tracker

Keeping track of how often you are activating your Freedom Keys can help focus your efforts. Draw this table in your journal (or download a template from www.bethkempton.com/flyfree) and fill it in every day for a week.

	Mon	Tue	Wed	Thur	Fri	Sat	Sun
Midnight–1.00am							
1.00am–2.00am							
2.00am–3.00am							
3.00am–4.00am							
4.00am–5.00am							
5.00am–6.00am							
6.00am–7.00am							
7.00am–8.00am							
8.00am–9.00am							
9.00am–10.00am							
10.00am–11.00am							
11.00am–Noon							
Noon–1.00pm							
1.00pm–2.00pm							
2.00pm–3.00pm							
3.00pm–4.00pm							
4.00pm–5.00pm							
5.00pm–6.00pm							
6.00pm–7.00pm							
7.00pm–8.00pm							
8.00pm–9.00pm							
9.00pm–10.00pm							
10.00pm–11.00pm							
11.00pm–Midnight							

Reference key

☐ Headspace + Heartspace	☐ Playfulness + Curiosity	☐ Boldness + Bravery	☐ Enterprise + Initiative
☐ Adventure + Aliveness	☐ Creativity + Innovation	☐ Connection + Communication	☐ Gratitude + Conscious Living

Using a different colour for each Freedom Key, block out each chunk of time you spend activating it in any way at all. Remember this is a Freedom Key Tracker, not an Activity Tracker, so only block out a section if you have activated a Freedom Key in that time. At the end of the week, reflect on how much time you managed to carve out, or how you managed to do regular things in a way that activated your Freedom Keys.

Keep on repeating this process, until a significant chunk of your week involves activating your Freedom Keys.

NURTURE YOUR DREAMS

When you start getting clear on what feeling free looks like for you, the dreams in your mind's eye will become clearer too. Even so, in the early stages these dreams are precious and delicate, and must be treated with care. You may have more than one seed of an idea, but until you feed and water them, you won't know which seedling is going to flourish.

It's your job to protect your dreams, and then once the green shoots start to show, encourage them gently with the support of a few carefully chosen people who have your best interests at heart.

~ Cultivating your ideas ~

Josie Adams and Tom Steggall met while working at a ski resort in Hokkaido, Japan. When the ski season came to an end they weren't ready to go back to their respective homes – Josie in England and Tom in New Zealand – so they took their knife skills and new romance to Ibiza, where they landed contract work as private chefs in luxury villas. While they both loved the adventure, they were serious about each other, so the time came to find a longer-term solution for being together.

The answer came to Josie in a dream – she and Tom could start their own mobile catering business, converting a van and taking freshly roasted coffee to holidaymakers and alpine festivalgoers in Europe's top ski resorts.

They packed all their belongings into their old car and drove from Ibiza back to the UK. On the way they stopped at Lake Garda in Italy and stumbled across a vintage gondola. They realized it could be a perfect home for their dream.

In all it would take nearly two years, many challenges and a lot of financial outlay, but The Coffee Gondola made its debut at The Telegraph's Ski and Snowboarding Show in London, ahead of its first season at snowboarding festivals in the Alps and summer events across the UK. By day it's a coffee house on wheels. By night it's a DJ hub serving espresso martinis.

'On a personal level, I've realized that following through with something and being true to your word is a principle I strongly believe in,' Josie says.

'Guarding our dream in the beginning was crucial for me as someone who puts so much store by doing what I say I'll do. It was important that we told enough people in order to get support, but not so many that I put myself under excessive pressure.'

Whether your dreams are small but beautiful, like a sliver of gold leaf, or large and lofty, like parachute silk, if you share them too early they will collapse. When a project is up and running it can be poked and prodded and generally keep its shape. It can go through various iterations, but hold together. A dream, however, is more delicate than that.

Exposed too soon, to the wrong people, your big idea can shatter into fragments. Materials scientists describe objects that break into pieces upon impact as 'frangible'. The first time I read that word, my brain split it into 'fragile' and 'tangible', and that's exactly what dreams are. They live in the hinterland between imagination and reality, and need coaxing to life. Too much pressure too soon and they turn to dust.

So give your dreams gentle attention. Let them know that you know they are there, and you are rooting for them. Tell them you're curious to discover more about them. Keep them tucked in a pocket for safekeeping, only to be brought out when you have a safe place to share, inside a friendship, with a mentor, or perhaps with your trusted online community.

YOU ARE ALREADY AHEAD

It's so easy to fall into the trap of comparison, especially with everyone else's lives so visible online. Even though deep down we know most people only show the shiny side of things, we can't help feeling that somehow we are missing something, we aren't quite achieving enough, our house is not quite beautiful enough, we are not far enough along compared to where we should be at this point in our lives. And if we shift paths, that makes us a beginner, and that's even worse. We are scared of not knowing enough, of looking stupid, and making mistakes. Being a beginner guarantees we are behind everyone, right?

Wrong. You are here, reading this book. You are taking action to live a fuller life. You are growing, and pushing yourself towards new things. You are open-minded and big-hearted, and you care about other people. You are here because you want to bring your best self to the world. And that, my friend, means you are ahead. Way ahead.

Not that it matters. It's not a competition. The sky is vast and infinite. There is no ahead and behind. No up front and out back. Birds are flying in all directions, from context to context, around the Earth and round again. Some are trapped, some are free. Some are flocking, some are alone. Some are soaring, some are nesting. We are all just birds, out there in the vastness, doing our thing.

Baby birds don't learn to fly just by watching their parents. They learn by trying it for themselves. They shuffle to the edge, hop forward, flap their wings furiously and hope for the best. Sometimes they fall, or hit something and lie stunned on the ground for a while, before they come round, shake it off and try again. They try over and over, gradually building their flight muscles, motivated by juicy worms and their primal instinct for survival.

In the end, it's the same for you. This is your life. It's about the joy and anticipation of finding your own 'juicy worms'. And it's about the long-term survival of your free self. So just concentrate on your own flight path, and let others fly theirs. You are ready to soar.

Chapter 17

SOARING: FLYING FREE

I'm sitting atop Glastonbury Tor, a place of pilgrimage for over 10,000 years. It's the day after a strawberry moon, a once-in-70-years occurrence that has filled the air with magic. Ahead of me, levitating over the Somerset countryside, is a huge golden-orange orb. It's a harvest moonrise, and as it climbs in the sky an elfin woman with flowers in her white-blonde hair starts to chant:

> *'Open my eyes and let me see.*
> *Open my heart and let me be.*
> *Open my mind and set me free.'*

The music seeps into my bones and I know. This is the call of the Freedom Seeker.

FLYING LESSONS

Through this epic search for freedom, across oceans, out in nature, inside dreams, through hundreds of conversations and thousands of hours of thought I have come to understand something fundamentally important.

I don't actually want to go back to being that girl on the holy mountain in Bhutan. I simply want to feel like her within the context of the life I have now. And I have the power to make myself feel like that anytime I choose.

What a revelation. No more being stuck in the past or wishing for a particular future. I have all I need here and now. It's just up to me to choose it.

And it's the same for you. Whatever feeling free means to you, you can take yourself there anytime you choose.

Don't get me wrong. I'm not pretending I have it all figured out. I'm not pretending that I feel as free as a bird in every moment, and that I now glide around serenely with two perfectly behaved children in tow. The truth is, if you come to my house you still might find me stressed or snappy or juggling too many things. But I hope that you'd see me catch myself sooner these days, stopping to join in the teddy bears' picnic, or laughing in the face of the chaos and sending thanks for the wonder of it all.

I have realized the depth of my love for my children, my husband, my life. I have expanded with the knowledge that sometimes my guilt and worry was an expression of that love, but that particular response to my context wasn't good for anyone.

I have discovered that there's no place more precious than inside a cuddle with my girls, but the best part of it is not the holding on tight but the stepping back, looking in each other's eyes and really seeing each other.

And I now know that when they look to me, I want them to see the free version, flying high. I have come to understand that my greatest gift to them is demonstrating how to swoop and soar, and inviting them to fly alongside me, wheeling and whirling in a sky filled with delight.

How about you? What have you learned?

Entry 28: Bird's eye view

Look back through your journal and see how far you have come. Take a few moments to reflect and answer these final questions:

1. *In what ways are you now living more?*

2. *In what ways are you now worrying less?*

3. *How are you now doing what you love? If you're still in the ideas stage, what plans do you have for doing what you love, and what can you do right now to begin?*

4. *Think about all the steps you have taken to feel more free. How do you feel in your body now?*

5. *And how do you feel in your mind?*

6. *What do you commit to doing in the coming weeks, months and years to ensure you continue to navigate to your essence, that place where you feel truly free?*

THE TAO OF FLIGHT

Look in the mirror once more and see how different you appear now. Do you know why? It's because that's no longer your trapped self, staring back at you. It's your reflection in a beautiful lake below, as you fly high above.

I see you as that bird in flight. You are centred and present and soaring high. You recognize all the forces that push and pull you, and now you are not flying despite it all, but because of it all.

Sometimes one force emerges stronger than the others – I watch you drop, I watch you climb. Now you slow down, now you speed up. Sometimes my heart goes out to you, as you beat your wings hard to make progress. And then I smile as a warm air current lifts you and you relax into the glide.

And now there you are, soaring once more. A precious perfect moment, your body rising effortlessly, your flight a beautiful dance.

You see, I am in the sky too, flying alongside you. I see you. You see me. I see me in you. I see you in me. We are in the same flock now and will continue this journey together.

Every now and then, you find a moment of perfect balance. As you fly in dynamic equilibrium you soar effortlessly across the sky, marvelling at the incredible view. This is the Tao of flight and it is the most precious reward of all. You have earned it.

The more often you choose to navigate to your essence, the more of your life you can spend in this place of glorious flight.

Entry 29: The Freedom Seeker's Manifesto

As your final journal entry, draft your own Freedom Seeker's Manifesto. Create a motivational message to remind you what is important to you, and why. Write a love letter that's going to reach you if you ever feel trapped again. Use words that will inspire you to soar. Look at it anytime you need reminding that you will always be a Freedom Seeker.

I have also created my own manifesto, which I would like to gift to you. You can download it at www.bethkempton.com/flyfree.

Print it out and put it somewhere you will see it every day, to remind you why your quest is so vital and the prize is so precious.

BE A BEACON

Your quest for freedom will be personal to you. But make no mistake, by finding what brings you alive, you will draw other Freedom Seekers to you, attracted by your light.

Whether or not you have children, the way you live your life can have a real impact on the next generation. As it stands, we are channelling people into an education system that isn't working. The people coming out the other end have false expectations, are ill-equipped for the real world and bear a huge burden of expectation, which they carry into their working lives.

So many of us are slaving away in jobs we dislike, sacrificing our precious time for things we don't really want and choosing our next steps based on someone else's version of success. Enough is enough.

We want the best for our children, and the children of those we love, and we try to encourage them, yet we often aren't modelling the advice we are handing out.

As a Freedom Seeker you have the means and opportunity to change things. Every single one of us can help others fly free, by flying free ourselves. We can inspire the next generation to be the truly free generation. And just imagine what potential that would unleash on our world.

FLY FREE, MY FRIEND

As one Freedom Seeker to another, I want you to know this:

Activating your Freedom Keys is a daily decision. Life happens. Things change. But you are now prepared and can always make that choice.

When you feel a stirring or a longing or a discontent, if you feel things closing in again, the colour seeping out, the shadows moving in, you know what to do. It may well happen, but now all you need to do is make sure you don't get caged again. Don't go back to your default mode of operation. Keep this book on your desk or by your bed and refer to it before the bars return. Try one Freedom Key, then another. Reach out. Check in. Do anything. Do something.

Remember, the good and the bad all passes, so experience all that is happening in the knowledge that it won't last forever. Be grateful for the beauty and breathe through the pain. Keep on going, keep on flying, for that's where freedom lies.

This is your life. You get to choose whether you live more and worry less. Whether you do what you love. Whether you stay committed to your path and to experiencing your life as your authentic self.

You get to choose who you fly with, or whether you fly alone. You get to choose how you spend your days, and whether you notice the moments of those days.

This promise is unconditional. You can choose to feel free come rain or sun, hail or sleet. Come calm days or stormy days. Through the tough and the turbulence, the rapture and the rebirth. You carry your Freedom Keys wherever you go and they will always guide you out.

Freedom seeking is a lifelong quest. It's an ongoing journey of awakening to what really matters, in the beauty and the dust. To what we can do, and to what we must.

Life is wild and glorious and hard and beautiful. We Freedom Seekers must keep choosing freedom with every decision, every detail, every dollar, every day. Because it's the experience of it all that adds up to a beautiful life. Go now and live it with all you've got. Fly free, my friend, fly free.

EPILOGUE

As I roll out my mat on the glistening teak floor of an outdoor yoga studio in Costa Rica one warm April evening, I have no idea that I am about to have one of the most extraordinary experiences of my life.

The sun is setting over the Nicoya Peninsula and I am taking a kundalini class. The circular rancho has a vast conical roof, held up by individual tree trunks which frame the jungle beyond. We are high up, perhaps 300 metres or more above sea level, and in the distance I can see the ocean.

The evening sun is sparking off the tiny dreamcatcher hanging round my neck, and hummingbirds are flitting through the trees. A pearly pink sky signals that the close of day is near.

In the class we are doing a simple pose, our hands pressed together above our heads, first fingers pointing upward. 'Reach for your life,' calls our teacher, Angie, unaware of the potency of her words. As I stretch up towards the roof I can feel myself crack open.

From the corner of my eye I catch something moving. A bird of prey is flying over the Pacific, now swooping, now soaring. She spreads her wings further, catching the soft breeze and gliding over the jungle.

She is a black hawk-eagle and I stand in wonder, watching her skate effortlessly across the sky. Closer she moves, silhouetted against the setting sun.

The class has moved on to a new pose, hands together in front of the heart. Angie tells us to think about how we are here, taking a yoga class at sunset in this beautiful place, and how, if we can make that happen, we can make anything happen.

Then the film starts playing, scenes from my life flashing through my mind: my precious husband, my beautiful children, the adventures near and far, the struggles, the loss, the triumphs, the friendships, the love, all of it. And I am filled with gratitude for every single thing.

I look up and see the eagle has come closer still. She's heading straight for us.

At the last possible moment this powerful bird swooshes right past the yoga shala, and in that second I am electrified, as if the eagle's spirit has leapt from her body right into my soul.

For a split second everything goes white. My heart is spun fire and tears are streaming down my cheeks. The sun blazes and the sky is alight. And then I know.

Finally, Freedom has returned.

She is me. I am her.

We are home.

⌒∼

ACKNOWLEDGEMENTS

How do you thank the people who have helped you write a book that it is the result of everything you have learned from all the roads you have travelled so far? How do you thank all the waypointers and guides who have loved you at your best and at your worst, who have made you see what's possible for your life? And how do you thank the many thousands of people in your community, who inspire you daily with their courage? I don't know, but I'll try.

My heart is full of gratitude for all of you, especially:

❀ Those who have shared crazy road trips and madcap adventures, precious experiences and unforgettable stories, opening my mind, making me laugh and gifting me beautiful memories: my brothers Jon and Matt Nicholls, Alison Qualter-Berna, Carol Couse, Chris Convey, Courtney Rumbolt, Dan Steel, David Phillips, Gillian Tabor, Heather Yates, Hidetoshi Nakata, Hilary Frank, Iain Ferry, James Nesbitt, Johann Koss, Kelly Rae Roberts, Ko Fujiwara, Kathy Heslop, Kristen Bromley, Kyoko and Michiyuki Adachi, Lara Schlotterbeck, Mrs Tanaka, Norifumi Fujita, Ollie Stone-Lee, Ricardo Betancourt, Ross McAuley, the late and much missed Matt Dunn, Tricky Turner, Val Lord, Yvonne Dawson, the Yamagata JETs, the ex-WCABJ crew, my UNICEF colleagues, the CCs of the

40th Peaceboat voyage, the England 2018 bid team, the Artful Journey girls, and the I Am Courage girls.

✿ The Freedom Seekers who allowed me into their lives and shared their stories so generously.

✿ My superstar agent Caroline Hardman of Hardman & Swainson.

✿ The dream team at Hay House, including Michelle Pilley, Amy Kiberd, Julie Oughton, Jo Burgess, Diane Hill, Sian Orrell, Tom Cole and Richelle Fredson, my wonderful editor Sandy Draper, and designer Leanne Siu Anastasi. There aren't enough words.

✿ Those whose generous insight helped shape the book: Sandra Cress, Lex Chalat, Frances Booth, Nele Duprix, Kari Chapin, Pia Jane Bijkerk, Duncan Flett, David Bull, Donna Gallyot, Esme Wang, and Professor Graham Taylor, Professor of Zoology at the University of Oxford (Jesus College).

✿ Lord David Puttnam, Kanya King, Joy Sander and Gail Larsen for being such generous mentors.

✿ Xavier Rudd for 'Follow The Sun', my anthem throughout the writing of this book. There's no coincidence it's from an album called 'Spirit Bird'.

✿ Emily Bett Rickards/Felicity Smoak, for an episode of Arrow that changed everything.

✿ My hosts as I was writing: the lovely folks at Costa Rica Yoga Spa, Bahia Rica Fishing & Kayak Lodge, Limewood, Berachah and Mettricks.

❀ Lilla Rogers and Rachael Taylor, my dear friends and business partners, and my wonderful colleagues – Louise Gale, Kelly Crossley, Vic Dickenson, Lisa Moncrieff, Rachel Kempton, Fiona Duffy, Joanne Hus, Reine Sloan, Rachael Hibbert, Mark Burgess, Margo Tantau and Zoe Tucker, who are a joy.

❀ My incredible Do What You Love community, for all of it.

❀ My precious Mum and Dad, who have taught me so much, and my lovely in-laws Joan and Bob Kempton. Thank you for taking care of my family while I was taking care of my manuscript.

❀ My girls, Sienna and Maia, who fill my days with sunshine.

❀ My husband Paul (Mr K), partner in love, life and business, and the best father that our girls could ever wish for. Your love has set me free.

❀ And finally to you, my fellow Freedom Seeker, for recognizing your cage and being brave enough to escape. We need more people like you, flying free and shining brightly in the world.

MEET THE
FREEDOM SEEKERS

I am forever indebted to the Freedom Seekers who have allowed me to share their stories in this book:

Alastair Humphreys

Alastair is an adventurer, author and blogger. He has been named a National Geographic Adventurer of the Year for his microadventures – simple, local adventures perfect for people's busy lives.
www.alastairhumphreys.com

Ali de John

Ali is inspired by anything handmade and everything cosy. She started a creative retreat called The Makerie to give people the gift of uninterrupted creative time shared with a loving community. She loves living in beautiful Boulder, Colorado with her husband and two young children.
www.themakerie.com

Alison Bartram

Alison never really settled at anything for long until the unforeseen death of her sister made her realize that today is a gift some never get to see. Alison grabbed an opportunity that gave her the freedom to surround herself with what makes her happy. Today she runs Heart Gallery in Hebden Bridge, UK. www.heartgallery.co.uk

Alison Qualter-Berna

Alison is a proud mother of three. She worked in production at NBC News and managed a global programme at UNICEF. After her twin girls were born, she created Apple Seeds, an all-in-one play space for children, overseeing three New York City locations and a national music franchise. She is obsessed with yoga and endurance challenges, and created the non-profit Team See Possibilities.
www.appleseedsplay.com and www.teamseepossibilities.com

Allan Girod

Allan is an actor, clown, storyteller, facilitator and the tallest husband Julia has ever had. Currently based in Perth, Australia, after venturing out for several years he has decided it is time to venture out once more, on a quest to reconnect and see the world through a different lens.
www.flaminglocomotive.com

AnneLiese Nachman

AnneLiese grew up in the wilderness of Pennsylvania, USA, forming a love for nature early on. With filmmaking skills from Penn State University, she combined her passions into outdoor filmmaking. AnneLiese resides in Seattle, where she and her dog, Humphrey, travel to the Cascade and Olympic ranges to create inspiring content.
www.anneliesenachmanfilms.com

Darin McBratney

Darin is a lifelong surfer and real-estate entrepreneur, who owns the beautiful Costa Rica Yoga Spa. After suffering a life-threatening illness, and playing an active role in finding a cure, Darin is now spearheading the Global Nurture Project, whose goal and aspiration is to 'change the face of modern medicine and healing'.

www.costaricayogaspa.com

Emily Penn

Emily is an architect turned ocean advocate and skipper. She has spent six years sailing around the globe exploring oceanic gyres – huge areas of plastic accumulation – through the organization she co-founded, Pangaea Explorations. Emily is an international public speaker and advisor on issues relating to our oceans, shifting mindsets and future society.

www.emilypenn.co.uk

Emma McGowan

Emma is an illustrator and surface pattern designer from Brighton, UK. Her work combines a love of drawing, painting and printing with contemporary colour palettes to create stationery, cards, textiles and illustrations that are fresh and decorative.

www.emmamcgowan.co.uk

Hidetoshi Nakata

Hidetoshi, a former Japanese professional footballer, played for teams in the Serie A and Premier Leagues, and for the Japan national team. After retiring in 2006, he travelled the world for three years. Since returning to Japan, he has been developing and providing opportunities to promote Japan's culture, crafts and artisans on a global scale.

nakata.net

Holly Deacon

Holly is a photographer and paper artist living in Hampshire, UK. Her world is in pictures and she uses inspiration from all

around her. In both her art and her photography Holly aims to create something that has lasting meaning.
www.hollybobbins.com

Jennifer Barclay
Jennifer is the author of *An Octopus In My Ouzo, Falling In Honey* and *Meeting Mr Kim*. A book editor and literary agent, she grew up in the north of England and lived in Canada and France; then she moved to a Greek island and hasn't looked back.
www.jennifer-barclay.blogspot.com

Jessica Hepburn
Jessica is the Director of Fertility Fest, the world's first arts festival dedicated to the science of making babies. She is also the author of *The Pursuit of Motherhood* and *21 Miles to Happiness: A Swim in Search of the Meaning of Motherhood*.
www.thepursuitofmotherhood.com and www.fertilityfest.com

Josie Adams and Tom Steggall
Josie and Tom run a successful mobile coffee business from a converted Canadian ski gondola. As coffee nerds, travel junkies and snow enthusiasts, they take The Coffee Gondola all over Europe.
www.thecoffeegondola.com

Karen Walklin
Karen's creative path is inspired by adventure and finding others who love the same. From Lincoln, UK, Karen is a wife, a mum and a grandma. She plays with mixed media art, and ceramics, and adores her motorbike. She loves mixing her favourite things to live a creative life.
www.creative-adventures.net

Kari Chapin

Kari is a bestselling author and champion of creative workers. She uses her skills to help people start and maintain creative businesses, with a focus on goal setting, time mapping and detail planning. She lives happily in the Pacific Northwest of the USA.
www.karichapin.com

Kate Eckman

Kate is an empowerment coach, motivational speaker and author of the blog, Love Yourself, Love Your Life, sharing inspirational stories about self-love, healthy body image, personal growth, beauty and fitness. She is also a certified Reiki Master, QVC On-Air Beauty Host and Wilhelmina model.
www.kateeckman.tv

Kate Hadley

Kate is the co-owner of Spinney Hollow woodland and co-founder of TreeCreeper Theatre CIC. She has always felt that creative play, connection to nature and the ability to be still are at the very core of positive development and social change. Kate lives off-grid with her two young children, partner and a variety of animals near Winchester, UK.
www.spinneyhollow.co.uk and www.tree-creeper.co.uk

Kelly Rae Roberts

Kelly Rae is an internationally celebrated artist, author, and possibilitarian. Her tender style of truth-telling and possibility-driven approach to life, work and art have been featured in countless publications. Her artwork can be found worldwide on all kinds of uplifting gift products. Kelly Rae also teaches a variety of popular online courses, and co-hosts the Hello Soul Hello Business membership site for creative entrepreneurs.
www.kellyraeroberts.com

Kerry Roy

Losing her job in her late 20s turned out to be a blessing in disguise for Kerry, who saw it as a sign she should follow her dream to create and off-grid glamping site. Inspired by her world travels, Kerry and her partner, Dave, created Camp Kátur, named after the Icelandic word for 'happy, in the grounds of a beautiful country estate in Yorkshire, UK. Having made a success of that business, Kerry and Dave are now beginning a new chapter in Abruzzo, Italy, with the establishment of their own venue.

www.campkatur.com

Kevin Carroll

Kevin is the author of three highly successful books. He has helped turn creative ideas into reality for many organizations such as Starbucks, Walt Disney, Nike and Mattel. Kevin has dedicated his life to advancing education, sports and play as a vehicle for social change and success.

www.kevincarrollkatalyst.com

Lisa McArthur-Edwards

Lisa grew up in Athens, Rome and London. She studied Interior Design before moving into Film Location Management, working on several award-winning TV series and commercials. Lisa moved to Australia in 1997 and started an events company with her husband, had a family and started a biodynamic farm. She later returned to her passion of art and is now a multidisciplinary artist.

www.lisamcarthuredwardsartist.com

Lisa Moncrieff

Lisa is a doting mum to Rosie, a little girl born with an incurable life-limiting muscle disorder. Lisa writes an inspiring blog and is practising life coaching to help families of disabled children find

freedom, positivity and happiness. She also climbs mountains and runs marathons to raise money for charity.
www.myweakmuscles.com

'Lotus' Juri Zalzala

Lotus is a freedom advocate. Having built a multi-million dollar business, he found himself living at speed and disconnected from himself. Regaining his health and joy for life through a vegan lifestyle and truth, Lotus now shares his freedom as a yogi, surfer, farmer, entrepreneur and artist, supporting others to realize theirs. He lives in Costa Rica.

Lou Archell

Lou is a writer, photographer and mum-of-two from Bristol, UK. Her blog, Littlegreenshed, features travel, botanical inspiration and practical advice on simple living. In 2015, Lou founded Sisterhood Camp, an annual creative retreat for recharging and empowering brilliant ladies.
www.littlegreenshedblog.co.uk and www.sisterhoodcamp.co.uk

Lucy Hill

Lucy works full-time in the media industry, but her true passions lie outside of her day job. From blogging about cultivating a creative life through the seasons, to having a passion for everything handmade, she's also a certified life coach and NLP Practitioner.
www.thepinkbuttontree.com

Mandy Henry

A fun-loving travel blogger, TV presenter and event host, Mandy took the huge decision to set up her own company and go freelance in 2012 to explore new challenges and experience life to the full. After all, 'life is not a dress rehearsal!'
www.travellightbulb.blogspot.co.uk

Nicola Moss

Nicola is a coach committed to guiding people to reconnect, follow their inner compass and create change from the inside out. She offers one-on-one sessions, as well as retreats in nature.
www.nicolamoss.co

Paul Kempton

Paul is a devoted husband and father, and a sports, film and comic enthusiast. After more than a decade in civil engineering, Paul made a major career shift to join Do What You Love, where he proudly leads a team delivering online courses that inspire others to find personal, professional and financial freedom.
www.dowhatyouloveforlife.com

Pia Jane Bijkerk

Pia is an internationally acclaimed stylist, photographer and writer, and has worked around the world for the past decade. She is the author and photographer of *Paris: Made by Hand* (2009), *Amsterdam: Made by Hand* (2010), *My Heart Wanders* (2011) and *Little Treasures: Made by Hand* (2013).
www.piajanebijkerk.com

Rob da Bank

Music broadcaster and tastemaker Robert Gorham, aka Rob da Bank, is one of the UK's best-loved music curators. He first gained attention with his club night Sunday Best, founded in London in 1995, which has since grown into a record label and three multi-award winning music festivals, Bestival, Camp Bestival and Common People.
www.bestival.net

Rohan Gunatillake
Rohan is one of the most original and creative voices in modern mindfulness and meditation. His company Mindfulness Everywhere is the creator of Kara, Sleepfulness, Cards for Mindfulness and the bestselling app buddhify. Rohan is the author of *This Is Happening*. He lives in Glasgow.
www.rohangunatillake.com

Sam Reynolds
In the last 10 years Sam has been diagnosed with breast cancer three times. Experiencing the far-reaching effects of cancer on many different levels, she set up Samspaces, an online virtual support network for anyone recovering from and adjusting to life again after cancer treatment.
www.samspaces.co.uk

Spencer Bowman
Entrepreneurial, creative and driven, Spencer has committed himself to building a people-focused business deeply rooted in the heart of Southampton, UK, as a catalyst for his personal mission: to see his hometown fulfil its huge potential.
www.mettricks.com

Vigdis Vatshaug
Vigdis is an eternal optimist and all-round positive person. Her passions are the outdoors and sharing the 'pura vida' lifestyle in Costa Rica with others. She is living the dream running Bahia Rica Fishing & Kayak Lodge with her husband, taking people out on the water to get an experience of a lifetime.
www.bahiarica.com

ABOUT THE AUTHOR

Nicole Le Bris

Beth Kempton is a writer and entrepreneur committed to helping women achieve their full potential. Beth's company, Do What You Love, helps people find personal, professional and financial freedom through online courses and retreats that are often described as 'life-changing'.

Beth is the founder of The Society of Freedom Seekers, an online club for anyone wanting to dive deeper into their experience of freedom seeking, in the company of like-minded people. The club offers an opportunity to access Beth's guidance directly, and offers resources and practical support for the journey.

Beth is also passionate about helping creative women flourish in business. She is co-founder of MakeArtThatSells.com, MakeItInDesign.com, online design magazine *MOYO* and the Hello Soul Hello Business membership site for creative entrepreneurs. She has been quoted in and written for numerous publications including *The Huffington Post*, *Marie Claire*, *Reader's Digest*, *Wanderlust*, *design*sponge*, *Sidetracked* and *Where Women Create*. Her online courses have been featured in *Flow*, *Uppercase* and *The Simple Things*.

Beth lives in Hampshire, UK, with her husband and two young daughters.

 dowhatyoulovexx

 @bethkempton

 @dowhatyoulovexx

 www.bethkempton.com
www.dowhatyouloveforlife.com

HAY HOUSE

Look within

Join the conversation about latest products, events, exclusive offers and more.

f Hay House UK

🐦 @HayHouseUK

📷 @hayhouseuk

♥ healyourlife.com

We'd love to hear from you!